THE GAP

WHERE LIFE HAPPENS

BY
KIM VENSKUNAS

Copyright © 2018 Kim Venskunas
The moral right of the author has been asserted.

No part of this book may be reproduced in any form or by any electronic or mechanical means, including information storage and retrieval systems, without written permission from the author, except for the use of brief quotations in a book review.

ISBN 978-0-987-0960-9-8 Paperback
ISBN 978-0-987-0960-2-9 eBook (epub)
ISBN 978-0-987-0960-5-0 eBook (mobi)

Publisher: https://kimvenskunas.com (Scratch & Co.)
Editor: https://wellversed.com.au
Cover: https://henryhyde.co.uk

A catalogue record for this book is available from the National Library of Australia.
1. Travel - Memoir - Self Help

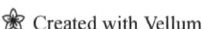 Created with Vellum

CONTENTS

That's Life!	v
A Question of Values	vii
Prologue	1
1. The Netherlands	3
2. Canada	23
3. Bali	41
4. Australia	61
5. Scotland	75
6. Spain	93
7. South America	121
8. New Zealand	141
9. Australia	165
10. India	173
11. Thailand	195
12. The Highlands	207
Epilogue	217
Old Proverb	225
Rudyard Kipling's If	227
A Note from the Author	229
"Bon Voyage, My Friend."	231
Acknowledgments	232

THAT'S LIFE!

I've spent most of my professional life in and out of work. On balance, probably more out, than in – not necessarily through choice or wrongdoing. But, as a result, there are some 'gaps' in my employment history.

During one of those 'between job' periods, a friend handed me an article from the Financial Times. The title yelled, "Gaps on your CV? Professional Suicide! Do anything, but don't have gaps!"

It enraged me. Intent on demonstrating the importance of gaps, I took to my keyboard. I battered out all the wonderful things I'd done and achieved during those enforced gaps. As far as I was concerned, the gaps are where life happens!

But, as in real life, things often don't turn out the way we expect. A year or so later, with the original manuscript in hand, an editor in my ear, and yet another gap to fill, I re-wrote *The Gap*. By which time I was ready to put my very private life into your hands.

I don't know how you've come to my story, and perhaps you don't either, but I sincerely hope you not only enjoy travelling with me but come to unlock the path to your dreams, too.

Best Wishes,
Kim

There are four questions of value in life,
Don Octavio.

WHAT IS SACRED?
OF WHAT IS THE SPIRIT MADE?
WHAT IS WORTH LIVING
FOR AND
WHAT IS WORTH DYING FOR?

The answer to each is the same.
Only love.

Lord Byron

PROLOGUE

As I entered the consulting room, the look on his face said it all.

"I've got it, haven't I?" I said. There was an awkward silence as the doctor gestured for me to sit and slid a pamphlet across his desk.

I scanned it quickly. Multiple Sclerosis, it said, was a difficult disease to diagnose. Symptoms vary daily and affect people in different ways. Well, that would explain why I'd been feeling fatigued, unsteady on my feet, experiencing pins and needles and numbness, slowed thinking and eyesight problems — symptoms mostly invisible to others, which was a problem because I appeared well to everyone else.

Dr George explained that 'sclerosis' — the scarring or hardening of the tissue is a lifelong condition that affects the central nervous system, brain and spinal cord — can take some time to get used to.

Diagnosis was confirmed. Prognosis — unknown.

"I'll see you in a fortnight. Make an appointment at the desk," Dr George said as he opened the door and bade me well.

I vacantly scanned the waiting area for my mother. I hadn't wanted her to come, but we'd done a deal – one, she wouldn't come into the consulting room and two, she wouldn't talk on the way home until I was ready; they were my conditions. I had a way of doing things – my time, my space, my way – it worked for me.

Mum joined me at the desk. I acknowledged her presence without meeting her eyes, a crisp nod. For what seemed like eternity we waited, suspended in space.

"How can I help you?" asked the receptionist.

My throat jammed. I struggled to hold back a torrent of tears, mumbled "two weeks," and walked away – legs like jelly – leaving mum to make the appointment.

Stumbling through the door, I stood in the street, lifeless and lost. There were no words. I couldn't face my mother. I couldn't face anyone.

"I'm not going to Venezuela," I sobbed over and over, as tears streamed down my face.

My dream was gone. My plans were over.

1
———

THE NETHERLANDS

Just ten months earlier I'd relocated to Leeuwarden, Friesland – the land of the black and white cow. Filled with lakes and parks, I think it's one of Holland's prettiest towns – like Amsterdam in miniature. I'd driven from Glasgow to Hatfield to Harwich, my car packed to the gills and my bright, shiny, new pushbike lashed to the rack. Across the channel to the Hook of Holland, north past Harlem and Amsterdam I drove, stopping only to stretch my legs at the Zeider Zee, one of the seven wonders of the modern world.

I was there because I'd become disillusioned with the corporate world. I was twenty-nine, living in Glasgow, feeling unchallenged and itching for something new. I longed for greater direction and purpose – an opportunity to soar. The world felt like it was pressing in around me – I was desperate to escape.

Then, one icy winter afternoon after a recreation studies class I'd taken on spec to lift my spirits, Dr Lindsey handed me a brochure.

"You're studying at the wrong level," he'd said. "Read that. If you're interested, get back to me."

It was an exciting opportunity – too good to say no, really.

Established by a Canadian organisation, the Masters in International Leisure & Recreation programme wasn't just ahead of its time, it was UNESCO sponsored. Since I'd first heard about the organisation as a teenager, I'd felt an affinity with the United Nations and UNESCO's cultural and scientific programs. Like many young people, I had been sure I had an important job to do in the world – one that would make a significant difference – and it was a dream to join the United Nations someday. I had an inquisitive mind, an insatiable appetite for new and different experiences and a desire to fulfil my potential.

The UNESCO-sponsored programme would expose me to a range of cultures and experiences beyond purely academic subjects. Thirty students from different nationalities were each carefully allocated to a house by gender, culture, placement interests and language skills. Each house would organise weekly social and educational events, hosting nights with visiting tutors and other community guests. I couldn't wait to sign up – not so much for the educational experience but the chance to find a purpose I could call my own.

I'd always been looking for somewhere to belong. My upbringing had been 'proper' – that's English 'proper.' Children should be seen and not heard, my parents said. Decorum and elegance was the order of the day. There were rules, rules and more rules, good behaviour, good manners, diligence and respect. Mostly, such demands stood me in good stead for later life. But they left their mark. I'd always planned to get away from England for good. The programme seemed the perfect solution. If nothing else, it would save me thousands of travel miles by dropping me into a different culture with ready-made connections, community and purpose – the chance to settle into a new life. I wanted to escape Britain, and this was my ticket to ride.

I didn't know how I could afford it but I had to find a way –

it was everything I wanted. I applied, was accepted for the next intake and was moving out of Glasgow in short shrift.

= > < =

I pulled into a newish looking residential area that would be my home for the next year. I'd been expecting a more welcome sight – something more like the enchanting historic buildings I'd seen as I drove past Leeuwarden's town centre. Instead I saw twelve drab two-storey concrete boxes set around a square, looking like the kind of pre-fabricated houses that had been built hastily post 1945. Timber window frames, splintered. Paint, peeling. Scraps of fabric hung at some windows instead of curtains, gardens were more like jungles. They looked liked they'd been unoccupied since the war but cars in the driveways told another story. My heart sunk – they weren't in the least like the typical Dutch house with an odd-shaped roofline, wooden window shutters and a colourful, well-manicured garden I'd imagined.

My eye caught the winter sun bouncing off a window behind the large overgrown tree in the corner. I plodded to the front door.

A six-foot-two hunk of physique greeted me with a burst of energy. The swarthy skinned Latino had dark wavy locks and a smile that beamed two rows of perfectly aligned, large, white sparkling teeth. His face was angular and masculine and he had a sunny warmth that lifted my spirits the instant his deep, dark brown eyes met mine.

"You've come for the course, yes? There's coffee on – would you like?" he offered as he gestured me inside. As he went to get me a cup, he fired off that his name was Luca, he was from Argentina and that he'd also arrived a few days early to settle in and prepare for our adventure. He spoke so fast and with such a strong accent that I couldn't find a space to get a word in.

As he rummaged in a cupboard I looked around the living room. Despite being sparsely furnished the large room had a lovely homely feel. There were two squiggy brown, cumbersome sofas surrounding a huge television and a Dutch seascape. Nothing was to my taste but everything *was* impressively clean. With full width glass sliding doors that led to the concrete paved courtyard, it was also a great party space.

"This is going to be great," I heard myself say.

"New to the Netherlands?" Luca asked, placing a coffee cup in my hand.

"No, I'm not," I chuckled. "I came here many years ago to visit my teenage best friend, Sasha."

"She had a troubled life," I added. "I've often wondered what became of her."

We'd had so much fun. Sasha called me 'Gonzo' after the muppet with a hooked nose – my nose wasn't hooked but it made her laugh, so I let it stick. I called her 'Topo' after Topo Gigo, the Italian cartoon character. Topo wasn't pretty, but her dark skin, beautiful smile and striking features were still very attractive. Sophisticatedly clad in expensive clothes and wildly charismatic, she looked older than her years, while I, blessed with good genes, looked younger. It's funny how we were so alike, yet complete opposites. I had a heap of brown wavy hair that hung half way down my back, until my mother got sick of using 'no more tears'. I wore my Lithuanian heritage on my face – bright blue eyes, olive skin, high cheekbones and square jaw. Unlike Topo, I didn't care much for fashion, but I took pride in my appearance – outwardly pressed and buttoned up, I quietly wore my confidence on the inside.

Topo had been sent to England by her Dutch-Indonesian grandparents, where we'd schooled together. I don't recall how she and I first became friends, but I do remember we made a good pair on the hockey field. We always pushed our luck – sometimes our cheekiness won out. Even when it didn't, we thrived on the challenge. That's pretty much how we were – well mannered, hardworking kids who knew what they wanted and were determined to get it.

Eventually, when her pregnant mother remarried, Topo returned to Holland and asked me to come visit. She and her stepfather would meet me at the airport.

Stepping off the plane, I'd teetered towards them, focussing on staying upright along the slippery airport walkways in my wine coloured strappy stilettos to offset my white outfit. I was a little taller than the average girl my age and proud of my athletic physique.

"I was a bit of a tomboy back then and it was my first foray into the world as a wanna-be young lady," I explained to Luca, telling him the story. I felt my smile widen, shaking my head in memory of that night. We were dropped at Topo's grandmother's house and told to wait until her mother returned home. But Amsterdam called.

The old Dutch house stood alongside a canal. From its huge attic space – Topo's bedroom – we could see the spires of Sint Nicollaasbasilick (Saint Nicholas Church) in the distance, protruding above the city lights. I'd desperately wanted to get out and explore but we'd been expressly barred from going anywhere.

"You've got everything you need up there with a built-in bar, fridge and record deck," her grandmother had said peevishly when I'd asked if we could go down to the end of the street. "There'll be plenty of time to explore later."

"Well, that was like a red rag to a bull for two fresh faced, impish teenagers used to getting their own way," I said to Luca. Feeling as if we'd been banished to the attic, except at meal times, Topo and I began planning obscure escape routes and plotting magnificent schemes to rid ourselves of the wearisome grandparent.

First we'd danced and sung ourselves into a fever pitch with

Frank Sinatra's 'My Way' on repeat – turning up the volume loud, then louder. Breathless and laughing our heads off we collapsed on the large mattress. Then we crept down the three flights of stairs barefooted to the entrance hall. We could just hear Topo's grandmother Annisa behind the closed door of the sitting room, listening to her Buddhist mantras and basket weaving. Topo carefully retrieved the door key from the hook beside the old wooden coat rack. The front door's lock clicked audibly – a short, sharp, solid 'tock' as the grandfather clock in the hall sounded it was nine pm. We'd synchronised it perfectly – the Buddhist mantras continued unabated. Slowly, quietly, we inched the door open until we could just slip through. Wide eyed, we sat on the step to slip our shoes on – we daren't speak. Then, hand in hand, we scampered down the street.

"There's a tram. Run for it!" I said pulling her along.

"No. No, we can't. We can't!" replied Topo with a strained voice. She pulled back. I tightened my grip on her hand.

"Come on!" I urged, "We've come this far. We can't turn back."

"We don't have any money," she wailed.

"We'll be fine," I'd promised.

Jumping on board, I positioned us next to the door, ready for a quick exit. We gripped the rail for dear life and sidled closer to a big group of travellers, hoping any one noticing us would assume we were with them. We rode for a good long time, marvelling at the city lights, but when the inspector lurched in our direction I pushed Topo out the door as soon as we reached the next stop.

The tram rattled away and we found ourselves alone again in the dark. Topo squeezed my hand hard in fear but I ignored her, dragging her behind me down the dimly lit street, remaining deaf to her insistence we turn back at once. I was drawn like a moth towards some lights pinned to an unbroken stretch of reddish brown brick buildings standing shoulder to shoulder to our left. Something appeared to happening there.

A dark alley came into view, smelling like a urinal. Peeping around the corner we froze against the wall – all mushy and wet with moss. There was a lady – in a window! Almost naked! It was a sight completely unexpected for two convent schoolgirls. We stifled a giggle as we took in her flimsy, bright red negligee and pale pink fluffy boa that draped down past the tiniest pair of black lace panties I'd ever seen. Her long shapeless legs were set akimbo, ending in shiny red stilettos.

She tilted her head, pouted and rolled her eyes – right onto us.

"Stront (shit)!" Topo called, pulling me back quickly. Giggling we ran back the way we had come.

"We can't be here," Topo cried breathlessly, when we finally stopped. "If my mother catches me…"

"How will she ever know?" I scoffed. "Besides, do you know how to get home?" I asked.

Topo shook her head, taking off again. I was tempted to go in the other direction – I didn't want to go back to that stuffy old attic. When would I get another chance to escape again?

Topo was rounding the next corner before I grudgingly ran after her. We followed the tram tracks for a while, not talking or even looking at each other. When we crossed over to walk along the canal I reached out to stop her.

"Why did you make me?" Topo hissed angrily. "It's alright for you. You'll go home eventually and I'll wear the consequences when you're gone." I didn't have an answer for her – I didn't really know why I was so desperate to explore the city. The idea of escaping had just seemed such a rush – as if I could finally see Amsterdam my way.

After what seemed like hours of wandering we were both cold and tired. It wasn't fun anymore, not by a long shot.

"How much further is it?" I asked, flopping down on a bench, determined not to take another step.

"It's only going to get colder," Topo said shortly. She looked back and forth along the canal. "It can't be that far now."

"Call your dad – I'm sure he'll come for us," I said, hugging myself to keep warm. Why hadn't I brought gloves and a hat, I wondered, feeling doleful and trying to brush the damp mist from my hair.

"No way! He'll kill me!" She screeched back. "We need to get in before Granny hits the hay or she'll call the police." Her eyes lit up. Taking off she called back, "Wait there!" reappearing a little later leading two bicycles.

"Where did you get those?" I asked astonished. "Did you steal them?"

"Be quiet," she hissed back. "Just come on. Everyone steals bikes in Holland."

We rode this way and that while I tried to keep up with her as best I could. Finally, Topo began to recognise where she was. She made us ditch the bikes a block away, sprinting the last metres to her grandparents' house. As we turned into her street, we could see her grandmother standing on the doorstep.

"Verdomme!" She cried when she spied us. "Kom hier je stoute maiden. What do you think you've been doing?" Topo cringed.

"It's my fault," I stepped up. " I wanted to go to the end of the street. Sasha just came out to convince me to come back."

Topo's grandmother shooed us in harshly, a torrent of Dutch coming from her lips. I didn't know exactly what she was saying but I knew it wasn't good. She pushed Topo up the stairs, leaving me to follow along glumly.

"You'll go to bed now and I'll hear no more from you," the old lady growled. "I'll be speaking to your mother, Sasha." With that she shut the attic door with a bang.

Topo ignored me as she changed for bed and slipped beneath the blankets. I followed suit.

"So, much for you and old Frankie boy," I said to Topo, as we lay as far apart as possible.

"Don't speak to me," she huffed, turning away.

"It was never quite the same between us after that," I told Luca sadly. "Our contact fizzled out after I went back home."

"Not everyone's made for adventure," he said.

"It was more than that, I think," I mused. "I've always been determined to do things my way – I've never given any thought to compromise." Glancing down at myself, I doubt much had changed. I was action girl. I was strong, athletic and up for anything physical from skiing off mountains with a parachute to scuba diving – the more challenging the better. I ran ten kilometres three or four times a week – I lived for activity and I was always searching for something more.

Somehow, though, over the years seeking had become all that mattered. As soon as I'd found what I thought I was looking for, I was off on some other quest. Restless, I'd travelled around the world looking for something to satisfy my soul, make me feel better, make me feel like the life I'd chosen was the right one for me. I'd left friends, family and lovers in my wake in my need to do everything my way.

"What happened to Sasha?" Luca asked.

"I don't know. It was evident our friendship wouldn't hold – I disconnected. I tend to do that," I murmured, my attention elsewhere. "I wanted to find my own path forward and didn't want to be pigeonholed."

"Did you find your way?" he enquired.

"No. I'm still looking," I said. "That's why I'm here."

We were interrupted by footsteps in the hall.

"Hola Paco," called Luca. " Pacquiao's from Puerto Rico," he turned to tell me. The newcomer extended his hand. With a sleepy voice he said, "I've been exploring."

Pacquiao wasn't your typical Puerto Rican, except for the gold wrist chain. He'd spent most of his life at school in the United States. He had a brown but pale complexion, dark hair and the darkest brown eyes that, in contrast to Luca', looked kind of vacant, as if there was nobody home. I suspected some kind of recreational drug. Nevertheless, he was an interesting character. He'd spent his summers working the Latino cruise ships, organising onshore tours and shopping expeditions, returning later, of course, to pocket his commissions. On board, he spent most evenings partnering the spinsters or wives of men who couldn't/wouldn't attempt a salsa, lambda or merengue. Perhaps that's where he'd mastered his acceptance and placidity. I was never sure whether Paco understood or cared about what was going on – he seemed disengaged. I must say he scrubbed up well, though. I could see why the old dears would have loved to cha cha with him – he had a raffish, boyish charm.

"So you must be rich, right?" Paco asked as he shook my hand.

"What?" I spluttered, almost dropping it. I took a deep breath, looked him straight in the eye and proffered my other hand.

"Hello. I'm Kim. I'm here for the programme, " I said curtly. "And who might you be?"

He laughed. "Hello Kim. My name is Paco," he said apologetically. "Pleased to meet you."

"So why do you assume I must be rich, Paco?" I asked, smiling back.

"Well, I think Paco means we're only here because we've got government sponsorship," Luca explained. "If I do good, I'll return home to a good job. You're looking at the next Argentinean Minister of Leisure & Tourism."

"And you think because I'm English I'm made of money?" I returned, harrumphing. "If only that were the case!"

I explained that I'd applied everywhere for funding but

finally my mum had re-mortgaged her council house so I could take up my place offer. While western governments, charities and philanthropists often offered grants or scholarships for students from developing nations, it didn't often go the other way.

"With the debt I've taken on to be here, I could well be in a worse financial position than you," I pointed out to Paco.

"Well, that's why we're here, isn't it? To change the world?" he said with a conspiratorial smile. I relaxed and sipped my coffee as he and Luca told me about their plans for the future. We discussed philosophies and politics, the pros and cons of communism, socialism, capitalism and fascism. We meandered around the changes we would make in the running of our countries. Luca particularly seemed smart, worldly wise and passionate about his country. I'd seen a fire in Luca's eyes – he wasn't on the programme for leisure and recreation. As he spoke, it seemed to me that the Argentineans were better off in many ways. Yes, they earned less, but then it cost much less to live. They had everything I had – housing, food, health care, infrastructure, recreational facilities – and while the quality and abundance of material goods may not have been equal, Luca suggested westerners demanded too much of the wrong kind of thing.

"My people are more interested in family, community and relationships; they could have more if they'd wanted – but they don't think it worth the sacrifice," he explained. It was true – I had been sorely lacking a sense of community and family in my life. I intuited that sense of belonging made him quite content with his lot, much more so than I.

"People are people, and we're fundamentally the same," I agreed.

"Really, we're both in the same position – just on different levels," Luca replied. By this time, I had high hopes he would be the next Che Guevera, not in the least because he bore a strong resemblance to the revolutionary.

That evening, Luca, Paco and I set out to explore the town by bike. We freewheeled, taking it in turns to call the direction as we approached each intersection – none of us had a clue where we were going.

We wandered around the town's historic centre, stopping to marvel at the millennia old buildings, windmills and tourist hotspots. I was enchanted. I loved the waterways, cobbled streets and beautiful buildings draped in hanging baskets, overflowing with brightly coloured peonies, pansies and others unknown to me. Which was odd, because I was generally ambivalent about flowers. I'd disliked them – especially roses, red roses – since childhood. One Christmas Eve, Dad had forgotten to get a present for Mum. My brother and I were hurled into the car as he tried to catch the shops before closing time. Mid-winter in the UK was dark, cold and miserable. The three of us ducked between last minute shoppers, casting our eyes left to the market stalls, right to the shop windows – desperate to find Mum a worthy gift.

"Dad! Roses! There's a flower stall!" my brother yelled, pointing the way. Hardly a worthy Christmas present, I'd thought.

"A dozen red roses, please," Dad said, hastily.

"No! Get the yellow ones. They're so much nicer," I suggested. Too late. We were off again. Dad, in his wisdom, hit the jewellers on the way out. He couldn't believe his luck – there was a simple gold pendant embossed with a single red rose on display and he snapped that up, too.

I'd felt deeply disappointed. I'd known red roses were supposed to say, 'I love you'. But, to me, he hadn't put any such thought or care into the gifts – everything had been done on the fly. I haven't quite trusted flowers ever since. However, now I gazed at the large wooden tubs filled with mesmerising bursts of red, orange, yellow and cream tulips that marked every intersection, I suddenly understood their appeal.

There was a circus in town — we thought it might be fun to go. Once in my seat, however, I suddenly remembered I'd left removable lights on my bike, which I'd padlocked with the boys' bikes to the A-frame of the lion's trailer alongside a stream of other bikes.

The performance had started, but I couldn't settle for thinking about the lights — I'd just bought them, along with the bike and its super dooper saddle. I didn't want to fuss. After all, I'd just met these guys. I didn't want to get them offside – I had to live with them all year. But I also wouldn't rest until I'd made sure those lights were safely in my bag.

Getting out from the rickety wooden stands was an obstacle course – too many people, bags and who knows what got in my way. The harder I tried to be inconspicuous, the more noise I made as I fumbled through. Outside, in the dark, I headed across the open field towards the wagon park. I couldn't see a bloody thing. Back and forth, I searched. Had I come out of the right exit? Yes, there was the lion cage, but…

All the bikes were gone!

It was a long late night walk to the police station. It seemed unmanned, but eventually, the desk sergeant appeared. I explained the situation as best I could in a mix of English and very poor Dutch.

Eyeing the three of us, he asked, "Where are your papers?"

I looked to the boys, shrugging, "What papers?"

"Passport? Visa? Identity Cards?" He questioned. "You can't work here!"

"Work? We don't want to work," I said, feeling like I'd been transported into a Fawlty Towers sketch. "We just want to report our bikes stolen."

"Where are your papers?" he repeated. Oh, no! Not again.

"What papers?" I rejoined.

"Bike papers," he replied. Okay, so now we were getting somewhere.

"Do you mean our receipts? Bill?" I tried to ascertain.

"Yes!" He snapped.

"We were out for the night at the circus. We didn't take papers. My receipt's at home and they don't have one," I said, increasingly incensed.

The sergeant looked suspiciously at my comrades. "Where did you get your bikes?" He demanded.

"We rented them," replied Paco.

"Where are your papers?" he repeated. For god's sake, I was losing my patience.

"You have rental papers?" He insisted.

"Non!" exclaimed Luca and Paco at the same time.

"Wait!" I roared. "Our bikes have been stolen!" Instantly I heard Topo's grandmother telling us: "What comes around, goes around, girls. You'll regret it one day." I shook my head, calmed by the memory and marvelling at how karma comes full circle.

The sergeant nodded his head – finally, he understood. But he didn't bat an eyelid.

"What did you expect?" he said dismissively. "They'll be across the border by now. It happens every year."

"You get your papers. Then come back," he waved us out the door. Clearly he couldn't give a shit. No offer of a ride home. No care that our transport had gone. What were we to do? How would we get to school? I was dumbfounded, then hopping mad. My brand new bike — gone! And nothing would be done. Welcome to Leeuwarden! But I swallowed my anger knowing I'd waived my right to complain with my actions twenty years before.

=><=

As well as Paco and Luca, our house was home to an

American called Zach from Sacramento and Finn, our Dutch host, who was vey helpful, kind and made a brilliant pancake feast before leaving us to our own devices at weekends. We agreed on a few house rules – the principle one of which was that I was nobody's housekeeper. We also agreed on respect for privacy (especially mine), acceptable noise levels (for us and our neighbours who were prone to complaining), but most importantly the state of the kitchen and bathroom. There was the odd skirmish but fundamentally our house worked well.

However, group dynamics, at the best of times, can also be a recipe for disaster. It wasn't easy living in close quarters with strong minded people from vastly different cultures – Moroccan, Indian, Pakistani, Middle Eastern, Israeli, North and South American, Polish, Romanian and British – more guys than girls and most in their mid-twenties to thirties. Throw religion and economic factors into the mix and we were almost a complete microcosm of the world and its issues. I was often cast in the role of mediator for some reason.

"I noticed you'll do anything for anyone for a smile," Rashi, the master chef from India said as a precursor for asking my help learning how to ride a bike. As stubborn as a mule, she persisted without adopting western clothing for an easier ride. We got there in the end, but she was no Lance Armstrong. Yet she rewarded my efforts with way more than a smile, giving me the most wonderful cooking lessons. For the rest of my life, I'd hold that time in the kitchen together dear to my heart. Selecting quality ingredients from local markets, preparing the fresh spices and marinates together made me feel like part of her family, despite them being in India. Plus we created a wonderful array of Indian dishes to feed anyone who dropped by.

Despite the challenges, I was beginning to feel like Luca, Paco, Zach and Finn were family. To be honest it was the longest I'd stayed one place for quite a while. In fact, it felt like I'd been constantly on the move since I was a teenager – most of it due to circumstances rather than design. First, the small convent school I attended closed down abruptly but three days after I had transferred to a new school I was back – the school's Governors in Rome had relented. By the end of the year it had closed again, this time for good.

"I'll get you a new hockey stick if you go back to Mater Dei," mum said. I agreed, but the hockey stick never appeared. And I didn't dare ask – I knew money was tight. Anyway, the one I had was perfectly fine.

Then we moved from Hertfordshire to Cambridgeshire, where my parents took on a pub called 'The New Crown'. Many a time I chuckled at the name – the pub was 500 years old while around the corner, The 'Old Crown' was, at a guess, 50 years old. I became accustomed to life in the Fens very quickly by playing hard, studying hard and attending to my duties at home and in the pub. Life seemed much freer – my parents were just too busy to bother about me.

Soon after they divorced. And my life was ripped apart.

=><=

During that first year in Leeuwarden, a new pair of tutors drawn from different countries taught us each week; one a world-renowned professor and the other an industry professional. The subjects covered just about everything leisure and recreation related — from the concepts of leisure across cultures to international policy development and application. It was hard work, but I could see the potential for a rewarding career at the end was huge.

The icing on the cake, however, would come in the second year – an internship in a culture other than my own. I spent hours dreaming about where to go.

My first choice was China. We'd had to secure a placement fast and within two weeks of arriving in Leeuwarden I'd been invited to discuss my plans with one of the professors, an American based in Switzerland who wanted to document the development and use of theatre along the Silk Road from London to Beijing.

Professor Joan was a portly lady who was based in Geneva. Her silver grey hair was styled to resemble a birds' nest – purposefully bedraggled – and it suited her. She must have been late fifties, but it was hard to tell. She reminded me of an old fashioned, round faced grandmother – sagging features, greyish white skin and deep lines that told her life story. She was unassuming, gentle and knowing all at once. I liked her.

To get to know her project more, introduce myself and create a good impression, I invited her on a day trip to Scheveningen, a cute traditional Dutch fishing port. We wandered through the old town before sitting in the bracing wind wrapped in padded winter jackets and eating deep fried mussels and chips overlooking the harbour. I don't know what I looked like, but Joan resembled an ageing mammoth. She listened attentively as I answered her questions, asking after my aspirations and how I'd come to the programme.

"So, what do you know of the Silk Route and China?" she asked.

I felt her surprise when I replied, "Quite a bit." My interest in China had developed as I prepared an undergraduate thesis in Glasgow. I'd even studied the language.

"You speak Chinese?" she asked, greatly surprised.

"I doubt I'd remember much," I told her. I hadn't wanted to raise her expectations.

"I'm sure you could pick it up if you were in China for a while," she replied. Was there an offer there?

Joan explained how theatre had been driven underground. Throughout the ages, during repressive regimes, the Chinese had used it to communicate important ideas under the radar. Her project sounded fascinating. I became excited about the prospect of learning something new, the risqué subject matter and living in a very different culture.

"Although our projects aren't exactly aligned, I propose you work the China element of my research while preparing your dissertation," she said.

Mission accomplished.

She wanted me to work out of Beijing. I would complete her team, joining researchers in London, Paris, and Geneva. Words can't describe how I felt – in the hazy distance morphed an absorbing, multinational team project with wonderful opportunities and responsibilities. I knew nothing of theatre in China but was determined to bone up on it as soon as possible.

Unfortunately the funding for the project never materialised and I was back to square one. But that was just the start of my bad luck.

Soon another option came my way in Perth, Western Australia. The project would use recreation to help the long-term unemployed back into work. Again, I became excited — with my leisure interests and corporate skills, it was a good match — and I would be learning and contributing at the same time. In Holland I'd begun to experience what it felt like to really belong – I suspect the warm blooded Latinos were responsible. Genuine and generous in their compassion and commitment to people, they made everyone feel part of the team. I'd stepped onto the first rung of understanding what it would take for me to truly belong. Would I find it in Perth?

Alas, I couldn't accept the offer — there was no funding to help support my living costs.

In hindsight, the failed Perth opportunity showed me how I'd jumped at China for all the wrong reasons. I'd lost sight of my real goal – to find a place to belong. I suddenly realised it wasn't the project that was important to me but the culture. Time was marching on with me getting no closer to a final place offer.

Luca and I had become rather close and I was beginning to

wonder whether Argentina might be an option for me. The first time I'd laid eyes on him, I'd melted. Then I got some good news. The student office called: "We'd like to see you – now, if you're available."

Dr De Vries had the stature of a stereotypical Dutch Santa Claus – soft, white hair (no beard), rosy cheeks and a welcoming smile. He always made himself available. He was a wonderful, charming man with a dream and had fought the bureaucrats every step of the way to create our unique programme. He genuinely believed in developing healthy communities through, leisure and recreation – healthy bodies, healthy minds.

I knocked on his office door and entered.

"Come, come," he said, pushing papers aside, and bifocals up. The look in his eyes, suggested he was going to tell me something good.

"What news?" I asked, playing down my eagerness to hear. I wasn't yet ready for another disappointment. Like many intelligent academics, Dr De Vries didn't waste his words on unnecessary details. But now he took his time to respond.

"I just received a call from Dr Vera Esteva. He's made a fully funded placement for you." He paused for effect. I waited on tenterhooks. "Please let it be Argentina!" I thought excitedly. I'd liked living with the Latinos – although their manana attitude was infuriating at times, their relaxed easy-going ways suited me down to the ground.

"It's in Venezuela," he smiled delightedly.

I could have cried on the spot. Never mind bloody China, Perth or the project – I was off to Venezuela! I'd had a lovely connection with Dr Vera Esteva, the old Venezuelan Olympiad. He reminded me of my grandfather – a true, old fashioned gentleman.

"Fantastic! "What's the project?" I asked, enthusiastically.

"You'll implement a sport-for-all program across the Pan Americas similar to the one Britain ran in the 1970s," Dr De

Vries explained. "If you don't accept, please don't talk about it. It's only for you."

Although, I wasn't exceptionally good at sport I had represented my school in a number of inter-school athletics and cross-country meets. Never coming last and rarely coming first, I thoroughly enjoyed the team camaraderie. I had since trained and coached at local athletic clubs, played local hockey, become a gym junkie and found solace on long road runs, but never marathons. I was a competent skier, despite the initial disaster on my first and last school ski trip when I ended up under the café tables as people relaxed in the sun after a hard morning on the slopes – fortunately my dented pride left the customers unscathed.

The out-of-the-blue offer was mine on a plate. This was it – committed to the public sector, providing sports and activities within a wonderful Latino culture, I'd made the next step on the road to belonging somewhere.

Then my luck really ran out.

2
CANADA

Without my knowing it, my Multiple Sclerosis symptoms had begun during my first year at university in Edinburgh – even as I was at my fittest and full of zest. Doctor's visits became more frequent, but they could find nothing specifically wrong with me.

"How's your personal life?" The GP asked finally, a little piqued. It was the last straw. I'd left enraged — I understood her insinuation. I wasn't a hypochondriac — I knew my own body. Something was dreadfully wrong. When I finally broke down and told my mother, she called my childhood family doctor, who agreed to see me straight away.

We discussed the minutiae of my symptoms. In hindsight, there'd been a pattern of strange incidents. Once, on a golf course, I'd bent to pick the club from the ground and, no matter how hard I tried, my hands wouldn't grip. I'd bent lower, frozen and embarrassed. Angry blood surged as I mentally shouted at the club to jump into my hands. Nothing. I laughed it off, telling the others to continue – I didn't want to spoil their game. I'd be fine.

In a restaurant, pizza in hand, pain had quickly intensified as swelling progressed up my arm. I'd dropped the knife and turned to my friend.

"You've had a stroke," he said, calmly but with a horrified expression on his face.

"Come on. Let's eat," I just laughed, dismissing his concern.

Soon, I ached all over. I wasn't sleeping. My body felt very old. An orthopaedic surgeon tested me for a range of conditions I'd never heard off — but no diagnosis was confirmed.

So I went off to Holland, feeling fine. Until the day everything went black.

It was a weird turn of events. Thankfully, there was no traffic as I pulled to the centre reservation on the dual carriageway. I turned to double check the way was clear – I hadn't expected to stop. Then my vision suddenly went black. I immediately, unthinkingly, slammed on the brakes. A shock of adrenaline rushed through me – I felt sick and weak as I trembled uncontrollably. Then, just as suddenly, my sight returned.

My first thought was a double-decker bus had blocked the sun. Impossible. One, they didn't exist in Leeuwarden; two, there was no sunshine to speak of this time of the year either. My second thought was "Bloody hell!" Then I put the car back into gear and went on my way. In retrospect, I think I simply couldn't believe what had happened. But I was spooked. I booked a flight back to the UK to see Dr George the week before I was due to head out to Venezuela.

He confirmed my worst fears. The MS had advanced. He strongly advised I cancel my trip. Faced with the decision to withdraw from the program or ignore medical advice, I was in a pickle. I'd worked so hard to realise the next stage of my dream – travelling the world. I didn't want to give it all up now – not for a bloody disease.

Each time I thought about quitting, I saw my well-laid plans for a meaningful future fade into the distance. Then, almost instantaneously, I'd find a reason not to quit.

"How could anyone know the course of this disease?" I'd tell myself. "Perhaps the MS will be different. Hell, I don't even feel sick right now! Why should I put my life on hold?"

Usually I had the courage of my convictions, but this time I'd been thrown a furphy – would I gamble with my health to pursue what I felt I was meant to do with my life? Mentally I exhausted myself, flipping from one option to another.

Finally, I drew strength from something my Grandmother once told me.

"What's for you won't go by you," she'd intone wisely.

And she was right.

= > < =

Shortly after I withdrew from the programme, Dr De Vries called with good news. Given my unique circumstances, the Board had agreed to waive the 'different culture' criterion and he had approved an alternative placement for me in Canada. But I would have to leave in a week to make the program he'd earmarked for me.

"You're not going, are you?" My mother cried in disbelief. I couldn't think why not. I shrugged my shoulders, pulled a face and nodded as I left the room.

"It's high time you grew up," she yelled after me in frustration. "You're in denial. You run away from everything."

"And who taught me that?" I muttered sarcastically over my shoulder. I was so sick of being told I was running away. I felt all the fear, disappointment and rage I'd been keeping in check for so long well up inside me.

"I'm not running away – I'm working bloody hard at staying on track doing what I most want in life," I called back adamantly. "Don't you think I know damned well I've got MS? It sucks. It's unfair. I'm scared. But do I have to let it ruin my life? No way. I'll take my chances, thank you."

Silence.

"What if MS never comes to collect, Mum? I'd have wasted my life, that's what!" I pushed on, daring her to challenge me.

I couldn't stop now just as I was starting to glimpse what my future might be like beyond the grind of a meaningless corporate life. I wanted my life to mean something. I wanted to do something that would help, even in some small way, to change the world. I was passionately committed to pursuing any opportunity that would support others to make things better.

I'd tried and failed so many times – I'd bailed on jobs and university courses for shiny alternatives I thought would better suit my goals. That's why my mother accused me of running away. Sure, I was often bored or felt advancement wasn't commensurate with effort. I wanted more, yes, but I was also prepared to work hard for it.

"You always think the grass is greener on the other side," Mum would say.

And I'd reply: "Yes. I do. And it is. Why shouldn't I have it?"

Though Canada wasn't strictly what I'd had in mind when I joined the UNESCO programme, I suddenly realised it wasn't the opportunity itself that drove me, but the search for something better.

"If I don't go, what has been the point of all this hard work? Should I let it all go to waste? " I questioned.

Mum said nothing but I could practically hear her furious thoughts.

"I'll think about it," I called to appease her.

Quietly, in private, I told myself I'd figure things out – I always did. "It's my life and I'll do it my way," that was my motto.

=><=

The steward called, "Ladies and gentleman, please fasten your seat belts and remain in your seats. There's stormy weather ahead."

Wrapped in Air Canada's soft, microfibre blanket, I was being lulled into a somnambulant state by the dull drone of the aeroplane's engines. I dozed, thinking about where I was going and where I'd been. It's odd. I don't have much memory of early childhood. The earliest I can remember I was about seven years old. I'd just let myself in after school when my grandmother had called from the kitchen:

"You've got a baby sister!"

Excitedly, I'd kicked off both shoes and hurried down the long hallway.

"Calm yourself!" Grandmother reprimanded. "And stay away from your mum – she's with the baby."

Even though it was long ago, I still feel the force of emotion like a hammer. Dejected at not being included in this momentous event, I'd snuck up two flights of stairs without a further peep. I no longer wanted to see my baby sister. She'd replaced me.

I think that was the first day I felt like I didn't belong. It was also the first time I remember suppressing my natural emotions and recoiling into the safety of my 'wee bubble,' as I began to call it. Over the years, it provided a little personal space of my own within which I could survive what I saw as my family's disinterest. Actually, we weren't what you'd call close at the best of times. Sometimes I questioned whether we were really a family at all – we were extreme opposites in almost every way, drawn together by a common history. It's one of the reasons I became addicted to travel – I was always on the lookout for a place I'd feel more at home.

School had been my first escape – probably because of Mrs Wooding. She was a lovely, gentle-natured, chubby Indian lady, always dressed beautifully in bright colours that accentuated her dark complexion. I particularly remember her presiding over a prettily coloured octagonal tin of dolly mixtures: "Little treats for little sweets," she'd say. The tin came out every day, but not for everyone – only one or two would be invited to dip in – a lesson in patience for seven year olds.

One day, Mum came to school to show off my new sister. The three teachers stood wooing and cooing, as if I didn't exist.

"It's all about her. She's the princess now," I'd thought. "Who cares about me now there's a new kid on the block?" Nevertheless, I did what I knew was expected of me – I kept quiet and out of the way.

Only Mrs Wooding noticed.

"Let's get the tin," she called in her soft, gentle voice. As she bent to open it, she whispered in my ear: "New babies always get all the attention. But they're not new forever." With my classmates gone, I got a double dip. Mrs Wooding had put a smile back on my face.

The age difference between my sister and I meant I generally played with my older brothers. We had our routines – every Sunday began with a two-mile walk for chewing gum from the old tin vending machine hooked on the wall outside the newspaper shop. We'd use the collection money Mum had put in our pockets because we rarely made it into church. We preferred to chew gum and watch the goings-on in the rail yard out back — before we'd got caught, that is. Weekly warnings from Sister Cyprian, the headmistress of St. Albans & St. Stephens Junior School had no effect.

"You're a disgrace to your uniform," she yelled, as I cowered.

She was sickly sweet to parents, but the nun from hell to us — "Stand in the corner with your hands behind your back. Face the wall until I say you can move," she'd say. Her punishments usually far outweighed the crime. It was a rap across the knuckles with the side of a wooden ruler if we misbehaved, or a slap on bare legs backs with a tattered old plimsoll — which hurt more than you'd think. I took the punishments – they didn't bother me at all. I'd so wanted to hate the bullying nun from hell but never could – I guess I didn't have it in me. Once I stood defiantly in the corner rehearsing for the school play, Joseph and his Technicolour Dream Coat – "… you can darken my daytime and torture my night. But if my life were worth living I would ask would I live or die, but I know the answers lie far from this world." And that's exactly where my emotions went – to another world, out of that woman's (or my family's) reach. Even now, years later, I loathe being told what to do. Anyone who says: "You should…" risks my ire. I want to do it my way, every day.

I was a naturally curious and studious teenager, happy to put my head down and keep out of the way. Most weeks I received a prize from Mother Velia, yet another religious book that would remain unread. Eventually I stopped posting credits — my parents never noticed anyway.

Occasionally it felt like I had a demon inside me — dormant for the most part but rearing up every now and then, especially in the playground. High energy and a mischievous nature weren't good bedfellows for the school's conservative environment and as a result I frequently faced Sister Paola, the most 'normal' of all the schools' teaching nuns. Her reprimands only made me worse — I would stand with my hands behind my back, while she performed her ritual — the habitual flat palm, forehead slap as she said in her Italian accent, "Is it possible?" I was convinced my real punishment was the stomach pain I felt while holding in my giggles until I left the room.

I liked her though… until she caught me on the roof retrieving the tennis balls she'd watched us repeatedly throw until they'd stuck in the gutter. The sight of Sister rushing across the courtyard, habit hoisted, yelling: "Get down! Get down!" is one I'll never forget. Before I knew it she was climbing the drainpipe.

I scampered as she doggedly pursued me across the roof and

down another drainpipe at the other end. You had to admire her gumption. My friends giggled as I was frogmarched across the yard by my ear and given the dressing down of my life outside the school office. But her own antics on the roof hadn't gone unnoticed. She and I each had a one-on-one audience with the Head that day.

Later, she took her revenge. School policy required Catholic pupils to attend the weekly on-site mass. Sister Paola had previously kept my non-Catholic status quiet — but from that day I was made to go off to church with the others, the better to become part of the flock. Inwardly I seethed, as I had to endure long sermons decreeing the proper behaviour for young ladies and enough "You shoulds" to last me a lifetime.

But when we moved to The New Crown soon after so my Dad could take charge of the local pub, I'd felt a pang for Sister Paola and the other nice teachers – in truth, they'd cherished me in ways my parents never did.

=><=

It was Sunday. The pub was closed after the lunchtime customers had departed and wouldn't reopen until the next day, which also happened to be the first day of my final exams. I'd been studying hard – it was important I do well. I had things to do.

Enjoying the relative quiet, I sat on the floor in front of the roaring fire, taking a short break to read the newspaper in between revision sessions. Suddenly my father appeared.

"What do you want to do with your life?" He asked cryptically, towering over me.

I raised an eyebrow.

"Your mother's leaving me and she's taking your sister with her. She said you can do what you like." And, just like that, he left.

I knew whom I'd choose instantly. My heart said 'Dad' loud and clear. However, despite dropping a bombshell on me at the worst possible time, neither of my parents breathed a word about their separation for weeks. They just carried on as normal. The business operated, as normal. Everything was 'normal'. Except when we went to the cash-and-carry. Mum excitedly went up and down the aisles acquiring new household items.

"It's for when we leave your father," she explained. "We? Was that the royal 'we'?" I wondered. She hadn't once spoken to me about her plans. It was the first time I felt like packing a bag and running away.

= > < =

If I'd thought Canada would offer a respite from my worries, I was sadly mistaken. The minute I walked off the plane in Victoria, British Columbia I was accosted everywhere by huge, brilliant red billboards with large, bold letters screaming at me, 'I've got MS, but it hasn't got me!' I was hit for six the first time I saw it. Slumping down on a bench I felt like life was conspiring against my efforts to go on as normal. Nevertheless, the words vibrated through every inch of my body like a mantra as I got up, plastered a smile on my face and made my way north to Malaspina University, Nanaimo.

A relatively small campus, the university was set at the end of a very long straight road on the outskirts of town. A modern concrete marvel juxtaposed with well-maintained grassed areas littered with students and lovely views over the small town and its quaint harbour was my first impression of the place where I would put to use all my UNESCO training. I was there to help create a 'One-Stop-Shop' for public services supporting Vancouver Island's youth. Youth services were predominately located in the north where the more affluent settled, making it difficult for those most in need to access. With triads, teenage pregnancies, homelessness, runaways from the mainland and drug and alcohol abuse rapidly on the rise in Nanaimo, I had my work cut out for me.

I was there to design and deliver a central access point for the town's troubled youth. We wanted to promote engagement without fear of judgement or rejection for everything from recreation and employment to medical treatment. I was initially responsible for research and development, but it wasn't long before I took a more active role meeting community service providers, heads of departments, councillors and ministers, all very generous with their time and assistance. My placement was unpaid so I was grateful when some of the smaller agencies offered payment for work over and above my project tasks. Whenever I could I offered to take visiting academics on cultural trips – it afforded me the chance to do my own sightseeing, fully paid. I would take professors on the ferry to the mainland, through the rugged Rockies from Vancouver to Calgary via Whistler and Jasper, returning through Banff, Lake Louise and the quaint mountain town of Kamaloops. The view from the glass topped carriage over placid lakes and dramatic mountains was truly breathtaking and it wasn't unusual to hear one of the professors cry:

"Bear. There's a bear!" And all heads would turn.

For local jaunts I'd start my tours at the picturesque, uber English style town, Victoria staying in the famous Fairmont Hotel so we could take afternoon tea in the Butchart Gardens, wander through shallow rock falls and the 800-year-old Douglas Firs in Cathedral Grove. Then we'd head on to 'the little town that did' — Chemainus — a coastal community founded thousands of years ago by the Coast Salish native peoples. I found the town's story particularly fascinating. In 1983, after 120 years of hewing its surrounding majestic forests, the last sawmill closed. Instead of complaining, the townsfolk went about remodelling their home as a tourist destination, creating stunning murals that showcased its vibrant past across the local walls. Now a tremendous open-air gallery, the Chemainus Festival of Murals is testament to how we can overcome adversity by creating something new and visionary.

I was keen to implement something of Chemainus' vision at 'my' One-Stop Shop. Engaging the kids to tell their unique stories through art was the perfect way for them to have a voice in a community that had all but forgotten them. The notion was close to my heart – I'd always had difficulty finding my own voice, whether it was at school, home or in my corporate life. Now, with the spectre of MS, it was doubly important that I continued believing in myself and my vision – who knew how much time I had to spare. I, too, wanted to be the little girl that could. I knew I'd made the right decision in coming to Canada. Majestic and untamed, it seemed full of wonder and possibility. I had so many reasons to count my blessings – I was half way around the world, meeting new people, occupied with purposeful work and defying my MS. Everything was finally falling into place.

$$=><=$$

Soon after arriving I found affordable lodgings near the university with a delightful, gentle and demure woman. Estranged from her son, Sam, Liz had a constant air of sadness about her. During an acrimonious divorce she'd allowed her husband custody, thinking he could provide greater opportunities for her son. She hadn't known he'd take Sam away to the mainland where it would be hard for her to maintain regular contact. Calling was futile — there was always a reason why her son couldn't get to the phone. Liz drew strength from her friends and her religious faith, hoping that when Sam was older he'd seek her out.

I couldn't help but see the parallels with my own life. On the day my parents left each other, I'd felt directionless and totally alone. Not wanting to endure a long, heartrending goodbye, I decamped to a friends' place at the last minute – no one was home so I just sat on their doorstep and cried. Nobody came to comfort me. No one even acknowledged my departure.

I was 16 and on the cusp of freedom, just beginning my life. I knew what life would be like if I chose to stay with Dad; I'd have been stuck in the one place. When the time came, I doubted I'd be strong enough to leave my dad – I'd always feel sorry for him. On the other hand, Mum was clearly the responsible disciplinarian. I knew that if I'd failed my exams she'd make me return to school. And I was terribly close to her parents and didn't want to lose contact with them.

Drying my eyes, I rode my motorbike to the agreed meeting point where I waited for my mother and sister to arrive, our car loaded to the gunnels. As they passed me on the A1, I slowly pulled out to follow them down the long straight road.

I hadn't seen my dad since.

=><=

Despite our very different lifestyles, philosophies and attitudes to religion, Liz and I developed a lovely friendship, often over dinner or coffee at the local 'Tim Horton's' – a popular Canadian coffee shop. She would regularly speak of how I reminded her of her friend Charles, who'd moved to New Zealand.

"When I talk with you, it's as though I'm talking with him," she said. "You two must meet. You're perfect for each other."

"Maybe someday, if I'm swinging past that part of the world," I'd laugh, thinking I never would.

One day Liz gave me a book called Catch the Fire, about a little non-denominational church set in a vineyard at the end of Toronto's Pearson International Airport runway. It claimed to be the place that, "God chose to meet with His people," with miraculous happenings supposedly a regular occurrence. I laughed as I read about the worshippers overcome with uncontrollable outbreaks of laughter, weeping, groaning, shaking, falling, drunkenness and behaviours described as a "cross between jungle and farmyard animals." Some swore their life was changed by the experience.

"Brilliant!" I exclaimed in jest. "If I'm ever going to find religion, it'll probably be at an airport. Who knows? Maybe I can court a miracle."

I saw a look of fervour dawn in Liz' eyes.

"I'll book us tickets for the weekend," she said enthusiastically.

True to her word, Sunday found us being covertly manoeuvred by a procession of conservatively dressed worshippers towards the airport church, their low-pitched voices a soft, gentle hum surrounding us. Pushed through double-swinging doors, we simultaneously stopped dead in our tracks — "What the heck?" Instead of the cute little wood church at the end of the runway we expected, we saw a massive expanse, filled with row upon row of plastic chairs facing a large, elevated, opulently decorated platform. Ribbons, bows and flowers were festooned the space — nothing had been spared beneath the vaulted ceiling's acute triangles.

We took our seats — centre back, on the edge of an aisle – not knowing what to expect. The gentle hum elevated as the congregation, predominantly white, filled the seats down the front. More people stood excitedly in the aisles. Liz and I turned to each other, both thinking how conspicuous we looked alone at the rear. The hat of a rather plump, middle-aged lady nearby took my eye – with her fiercely waggling hand I couldn't tell whether she was scolding a young boy in cowboy boots and a flocked farmer's shirt (they were all the rage at the time), or whether she was anointing him. The crowd looked a little scary, actually.

An elevated hubbub broke out near the stage. "Praise the Lord!" boomed about the room – and I ducked involuntarily. It was the loudest noise I'd ever heard in a church. The congregation – a raucous, jubilant throng – swung into action. Arms flayed, bodies gyrated uncontrollably. A talented band of youngsters bashed out loud rock music on the stage. I couldn't believe my eyes.

Suddenly, all around us, people fell to the floor. The minister called for those who wanted healing and I immediately felt compelled to comply. Before you could say 'Jack Rabbit,' Liz and I were standing before the pulpit for a 'laying of hands.'

"Please give healing for MS," Liz mumbled quickly as the minister's hand rose, stopping just short of my forehead. My eyes widened as she began babbling in tongues – a language-like rhythm that resembled speech but only superficially. It was incomprehensible to me, but oddly comforting. I knew that glossolalia or xenogolossy was a sacred language that the Apostle Peter had declared was the fulfilment of prophecy — that it was the sign of God pouring his Spirit upon all flesh.

At that moment the strangest sensation came over me; my head felt light, my chest and shoulders succumbed to a weakness that sank to my legs. I resisted the desire to fall backwards. There was no way I could lose control here in this place of mayhem.

Then it was over.

"Come again, when you're ready," the Minister said, turning away to another supplicant.

I staggered back to my seat, half bemused, half incensed, perhaps a little hopeful. Had I got my miracle? I guessed only time would tell.

=><=

and, apropos of nothing, said: "Cor! That's a bloody good job. An accountant."

He looked directly at me.

And a light kind of turned on. I was good with numbers — that's what I could do. Immediately reached for the yellow pages next to the phone on the hall table and began systematically cold calling local accountants until one agreed they'd consider me as a trainee. The next day I fronted up to the office suited and booted in my smart new clothes. I was shown into a ground floor office with a huge Victorian sash window overlooking a quaint garden courtyard.

"This is where you'll be working," my new boss said gruffly. He must have seen my reaction – it was better than I'd expected.

"You're here to work, not stare out the window all day," he growled, as he removed the calculator. "And you won't be needing this."

What had I let myself in for? I sat down at the desk and defiantly stared out the window. Then I remembered an old family legend – my grandad's brother had apparently been able to simultaneously add two columns of figures in the old-style ledgers as he ran his fingers up the page. He hadn't needed a calculator – maybe I'd inherited the gene.

'Fine, I'll do the same,' I thought, stubbornly. And that's how I chose a career in finance.

Being able to deliver my Granddad's ol' mukker such joy made me feel close to my grandparents for a few moments, in mind if not in body. The few hours I spent in Bill and Betty's company had been quite special – I'd felt connected, like I was part of a big, friendly family.

=><=

Do you know the saying: "Eternity is like time; too quick for those who love and too slow for those who wait?" The time I

At the behest of my grandfather, I'd tracked down his friends, Bill and Betty, who'd immigrated to Canada from the UK a lifetime ago. I was too young to remember them, but they remembered me. I was proud as punch that my grandparents had entrusted me to their friends. Bill was a local market gardener who had been an early customer of Granddad's store in England. They'd lived on opposite sides of a wood and their shared stories had been interwoven into my childhood like folklore. Now, after a major stroke, Bill was severely disabled, his speech difficult to understand. I held out my hand to introduce myself when he burst into laughter and his eyes sparkled mischievously. Betty interpreted for me – he'd said: "You've got to be a Carter."

"Well, I'm not. But my grandmother often thought so," I laughed. "She kept forgetting Grandad wasn't my father." It made me feel warm and loved when she did, as if she thought of me more as a daughter. And, in truth, I'd often felt she and Grandad were more parent-like than my own.

My grandfather had been so instrumental in my formative years. Before my parent's divorce I'd toyed with becoming a vet, but that was looking more unlikely with my 'O' Level results. After my father had left, I was haunted by his words to me that night before my exams. What did I want to do with my life? I'd never really had a plan; we didn't really talk much about careers in those days. Or maybe I was just one of those kids who simply fell through the gap. I'd just wanted to make my parents proud and I was certain I'd be the consummate professional whatever I chose to do. What that would be, though, was far less clear to my 17 year old self.

So I was grateful when my grandparents arrived on holiday from Australia. One day, I was sitting at the bottom of the stairs, contemplating whether to do more study or maybe just get an entry level job somewhere when Grandad returned from an early meeting with his accountant. He opened the front door, saw me spent in Vancouver Island passed far too quickly. I had truly felt at home; I'd wanted to stay and see the work I'd done on the One Stop Shop to its conclusion. But my visa was up – I would have to leave and reapply if I wanted to come back.

A beautiful thing happened to me the day before I left. It had been a sensational autumn day, the trees shrouded in beautiful warm hues of red, yellow, orange and gold. My usual morning walk to school would either take me along the riverside or through the plantations and across the brooks — a perfect start to the day. But that morning I'd opted for the bus.

As I waited pensively, an Inuit took a seat at the other end of the bench. He returned my smile then bent to pick something from the ground. He reached towards me, offering a small white feather.

"He flies with the eagles," he said.

That evening I received word my grandfather had died.

===><===

3

BALI

Whether he 'knew' of my grandfather's death or no, that stranger's kind gesture stayed with me. I later learned the indigenous peoples of the Arctic regions hold the eagle in the highest regard. And, from that day forward, I also took the eagle as my symbol.

Granddad's strong, slender build, soldier-like stance and pale blue eyes gave the impression he was as straight as a die. You certainly knew where you stood at any time. I was acutely aware of his thin hands and long index finger, as he frequently used it to set me straight. That said, he was a gentle man in every sense of the word. I don't recall him being warm or affectionate but I can't say he wasn't, either. To me, he was just lovely – a sentiment I suspect many granddaughters share about the grandfathers.

The eldest child of four, my mother always spoke about Granddad's 'other side.' After the war, it had taken a while for him to contain his rage. He'd been a R.E.M.E. (Royal Engineers) Sergeant through North Africa and Dunkirk, fortunate to return uninjured (physically), unlike many of his men. In my grandmother's bad books, he was Ernest, and Ernie – the fastest milk cart driver in the west – the rest of the time. He presided over what we would call today a 'deli' — he and my grandmother were purveyors of fine foods, you could say. Granddad had worked in the grocery trade most of his life; as a young man he made deliveries on an old-fashioned cycle with sit-up-and-beg handlebars, a wicker basket, and a sign bearing the company name attached to the frame. Rumour has it that out on his rounds he often saw a spritely young thing — recognisable by her knickers as she performed handstands against the wall. You guessed it – that was my grandmother, Yvonne, his perfect match.

Born into an English-Irish army family based in Burma and later Gibraltar, she was proud of her 'hopeless father', as she referred to him, simply for being photographed with King George VI. Later in life she was the polar opposite to my grandfather physically – a portly lady, well groomed, but never over dressed. She mostly wore pants (I suspect I inherited my tom-boyish ways from her) and she was a keen sports woman, and a good one in her day. She really was the equal of my grandfather – strong, pragmatic and forthright. She stood no nonsense and always gave a good rational, logical solution to any problem.

Over the years I'd spent quite a lot of time with my grandparents. My mum was young and inexperienced, and needed a helping hand because my father was away for work a lot of the time. It was probably easier for her to manage the two boys, and eventually the baby, without me. My earliest memory of my grandfather was being in the flat above his shop waiting for Mum to finish his home deliveries. Granddad always found work for 'the devils hands.' In the back, where sides of bacon hung wrapped in thick white muslin cloth, he had me stand watching the little white box buzzing above my head, waiting for the 'cuckoo clock-style' fly swatter to SWAT those dastardly flies away.

"Anything to report?" he'd call from the front of the shop. Humph, not likely, I'd think. But I'd keep a watch anyway.

When my grandparents retired, I spent many a school holiday with them at Ubbeston Green, Suffolk where my grandfather sold Sprats dog food — I'm sure Nan suggested 'chewing the fat' part-time with the farmers to get him out the house and from under her feet. Every day, Granddad and I walked the dogs for miles across fields that ran up to the back of their bungalow — Kelly, the crazy Irish Water Spaniel and Diddles, the even more crazy toy poodle. One day I stopped him, dead in his tracks. It was a cold misty evening, the sods hard with frost and I was convinced I could see a horse's head hanging in the tree before me. Despite there being no such thing, I wouldn't let it go, certain the Godfather must be in the neighbourhood. He kept that story alive for years to tease me.

He was a good, fair but tough man who did me a lot of favours, though it might not have seemed so at the time. I remember he'd grip my wrist as I cleared then wiped the table, gently whispering, "If a job's worth doing it's worth doing well. Now, fetch the cloth and do it properly." Many a time since, I've subconsciously heard him utter those words and taken a good hard look at whatever I happened to be doing.

As I matured so did Granddad's tales. One night, late after the family had gone to bed, he told me his war story. I listened closely while his eyes welled — when he was offered another tour my grandmother forbade him to accept, for he had a young family and had done his bit.

"I owe my life to your grandmother," he'd say. Not one of his battalion survived the second tour. "Why me? Why did I survive? I've asked myself that constantly over the years." And he'd stare at me, as if I could answer.

"You had to be here for me," I suggested cheekily, attempting to lighten the mood. And he'd smile and give me a gentle tap on the shoulder.

I had a special connection with my grandparents; I thought of them, rather, as parents. I loved them, wholeheartedly and I believed they loved me, too. In later years, an American cousin told me, "You're definitely their favourite." I knew it to be true. But, I suspected it just was because I'd kept in touch when they'd emigrated to Australia.

"Jac, what do you think of Australia?" My grandfather had asked my mother, out of the blue.

"Dad, you go. You've seen my kids grow up. You should go see my little sister's kids grow up in Melbourne," she replied with a lump in her throat. She hadn't wanted them to leave England. They were her security. I didn't want them to go either – they were my mates. And I had just reached the age when I could visit on my own accord. Finally eligible for a driving license and my grandparents would be gone! Who would I talk to? Who would care for me now?

=><=

My bright, bubbly personality and permanent smile had completely disappeared. I was rudderless, confused and about to embark upon adulthood, sorely in need of parental support and guidance. Neither was forthcoming, physically or emotionally. Feeling responsible for my mother and sister, I adopted an adult role for which I was ill equipped.

My desperately-needed shoulder to cry on came sooner than expected in the form of a local lad – not really my type, but he was kindly. I was mesmerised by his pure white hair, tanned skin and a body builder physique that was the result of his job as a labourer. Plus his timing was perfect – or so I'd thought. One night, though, when he was walking me home, he turned on me viciously for no apparent reason, giving me a black eye. A while later we were waiting for my mum in my little white-topped blue mini. She was running late — and he took that opportunity to turn on me again as though the waiting was my fault. My head bounced off the metal hook and my lip split. The dark of the winters' night made it easy to obscure the injury from my mother — until the light of the next day.

"Why don't you go to Australia, see my mum and dad?" She asked. "You're 17 now – old enough to travel on your own."

I didn't really care if my problems were being shipped out of the way again. I took my chance to get away and booked my ticket. You might think visiting grandparents isn't the act of a wildly adventurous independent traveller. And you'd be right if it weren't for the fact that I sneakily added a quick stopover in Bali on the way to Melbourne.

And just as well that I did. I learned three great life lessons in Bali, even if I didn't fully realise their significance until later.

=><=

When I touched down in 1981, Bali's mountains, sandy beaches and rugged coastline, lush rice terraces and barren volcanic peaks all provided a picturesque backdrop to a deeply spiritual and unique culture. Known as the Island of the Gods, it was a popular tourist destination even then (particularly with Australians). Its surf beaches, bars, yoga and retreats were legendary.

Despite my late afternoon arrival it was dark, hot and humid. Not a breath of air to be had anywhere. Stepping out from the airport building was like withstanding a furnace. I was instantly soaked in sweat. Intoxicating odours confused my sense of smell — were they pleasant or not? I couldn't tell. The assault on my senses was like nothing I'd ever experienced – all extremes and opposites, wonder and discomfort simultaneously.

My first lesson came quickly – when running to another country, never let kind people do things without asking, 'how much?' Zapped by the humidity I couldn't stand my ground when without so much as 'by your leave' porters took my luggage to a hotel's shuttle bus, divesting me of my money along with my bags. I'd booked a rather nice place for my first solo, overseas trip; perhaps the bus was a free perk? I followed wearily and spent an anxious bus ride wondering where I was going and how long the cash I had with me would last. I'd brought limited money – it was supposed to be a quick stopover – just a look round and on to Melbourne.

The bus deposited me on the tropical peninsula at Nusa Dua, a magnificent open-fronted sandstone hotel that showcased Bali's rich architectural traditions — grand spaces, intimate corners, ornate pavilions and crystal clear lagoons. As I stood waiting to check-in, the jasmine-fragranced breeze refreshed me as it wafted through acres of colourful, tranquil gardens running down to the beach — I couldn't help but think it looked like paradise.

"Lady, you want to check-in?" asked the petite, delicate faced receptionist. She was so pretty and immaculately presented in her well-fitted, sky blue, gold trimmed uniform – not a bead of sweat to be seen.

Embarrassed by my ill-fitted, sweat-soaked travel clothes, I stepped forward.

"Yes, please," I said, presenting my passport.

"Room for one?" she asked. At the flick of her wrist a porter arrived.

"You have personal porter?" she said, as he lifted my rucksack onto his trolley.

"No. No," I said in a panic. "I don't want a porter. I can carry my own bags, thank you."

"Yes. It's okay. Don't worry," she tried to assure me, "Everything's okay. He stay with you."

"Stay with me?" I didn't understand what she meant. I hadn't ordered a personal porter, I couldn't afford it and I didn't want a young boy staying with me – well, not this young guy. He was too young – and too thin.

"For solo travellers, the hotel provides a complimentary personal porter — a young boy — to fetch and carry on request," the head receptionist clarified in perfect English.

"Should you require anything, just ask. He is responsible for ensuring your comfort and safety — when you retire he will sit on the floor outside your room for the entire night – he is at your service," she added.

Wow! I couldn't believe my ears – had I heard correctly? Not one hour after arriving in a new culture I was being taken care of for what felt like the first time in my life. It was an uncomfortable feeling.

I hadn't realised, until I sat on the edge of the bed, how much the humidity affected me. I was exhausted. I showered and curled up in the big, inviting bed.

Startled out of a deep sleep, I looked at the clock – only two in the morning? I tossed and turned, without peace. Then I thought I'd heard someone at my door. I quickly whipped clothes on and peered through the eye-glass. Nobody there. But I'd definitely heard a noise. I opened the door – 'slowly, slowly, catchy monkey,' I'd thought, just as my grandfather often said. I took a step out into the hall, and yelped as I felt something beneath my feet topple me over.

A tiny boy was curled like a cat at my door.

"Oh, Madam. So sorry, Madam. Please. Please," he said, trying to pull me up. "I get help – you have blood."

"Blood? Where?" I asked, placing my hand on my head. I pulled it away to see a stain of red but it was already drying.

"No. No. Don't worry. She'll be fine," I said dazedly staggering backwards into my room and shutting the door. Strangely, after that I slept quite soundly.

For breakfast there was a splendid array of fresh fruit and

other delights, presented with the utmost finesse along the buffet trestles so you could help yourself.

"Amazing. I don't want to spoil it," I said to nobody in particular.

"Incredible. It doesn't look real. So delicate and artistically presented," replied the lady beside me.

"Where are you from?" I asked, without waiting for a response. "Italy?"

"I noticed you check-in. Are you travelling alone?" she asked. I was a little hesitant to answer.

"Please, you should join us," she entreated. "We're going sight-seeing today. It's Ramadan — and the island's Muslims are celebrating." She gestured to her husband over by the window. You know those couples that look as if they should be together? Like brother and sister, but not? These two could have been twins. They were equally tall, lightly tanned, with matching bright cocoa eyes and smiles that said they were in love. Both wore pale khaki, zip-off safari pants with simple, plain crewed necked T-shirts – his dark khaki and hers charcoal, with a patterned silk scarf, azure and white, elegantly wrapped around her nape. They looked about ten or more years older than me and I felt at ease in their company at once.

I brimmed with satisfaction. I was in an amazing hotel, with a personal porter. And now I'd made friends. But we certainly got more culture than we'd bargained for.

"Would you like to make an offering?" asked our guide. The unspoken consensus, as I read it, was 'No way' but all three of us nodded in unison. I felt it best to respect the local cultural and religious beliefs.

"Follow me," the guide told us as he slipped his shoes off at the bottom of the steps. That was bad enough. 'My feet? My delicate bony feet – bare – in that shit?' I felt sick. I kept thinking, 'I don't want to do this,' over and over. But I moved forward regardless, as he demonstrated how to put our hands deep into a bowl of disgusting smelling green-black gruel. I lifted a glop of cold, thick sludge in my cupped hands and plonked it in the middle of a jungle leaf, wrapping this in a chequered cloth then pinning it with a bamboo stick, just like the guide showed me. The offering was to be placed beside a very primitive looking stone idol. I couldn't believe what I was doing – making an offering to a stone idol, let alone the gruel. I drew a line at saying a prayer.

We must have done a good job because our guide seemed to think we were keen to stop and make offerings to every idol along our route – and there were hundreds. We saw little else. After a good five hours of repeating the disgusting routine at every sacred spot, I'd developed a Pavlovian reaction to the sight of a stone idol, any stone idol and I'd determined never to agree to something I didn't want to do ever again, just for the sake of politeness.

Finally, we were free to stroll along the pitted market strip, sheltered from the direct heat of the late afternoon sun by gently quivering, glistening leaves. It was too risky to loiter — the hawkers were persuasive, calling for us to peruse their brightly coloured wares, leather goods, trinkets and the ever-present street food. The smell of spicy chicken cooking over coals was hard to resist, despite being mauled by hands better suited to rice paddies. We refuelled as we took in the spectacular vista across the ocean to one of Bali's 'not to be missed' Hindu shrines, the famous Pura Tanah Lot Temple, the 'Land in the Sea' – three acres of rock shaped by the constant battering of tidal waves. We learned that in the fifteenth century a high priest called Niratha had come there to spread Hinduism. He'd rested on the rocky island and later convinced local fisherman to build a shrine there to worship the sea god, Baruna. As he shared his teachings from the shrine, the village chief gathered men to dispel him. The legend says Niratha resisted by shifting the large rock – Tengah Lod – he was meditating on out to sea while turning his sashes into sea snakes to guard his back. Humbled by the priest's powers, the chief vowed allegiance.

I felt a strange affiliation with the story. I'd felt like I, too, was a rocky outpost adrift in a wide ocean, battered not by a tidal wave but a boyfriend. My family had cast me out to sea, over to the other side of the world. What power would look after me, here? Who would offer me a blessing? In that moment, with salt spray cooling my face, I decided to rely on no body but my own. I'd lay no more wreaths and make no more offerings at the foot of any man or icon. I would be responsible for me. And, if there was a God, he could talk directly to me – I'd accept no intermediaries.

$$=><=$$

The next day, I ventured north to Ubud where I found a secluded room at traditional hotel with a thatched roof, local stone and timber walls, an oversized timber deck and a crystal clear, turquoise pool. As I put my shoulder to a very heavy solid wood door in a brushed wood fence that would have looked right at home in a monastery, I peered through to see what my 800,000 rupiah had bought me. I lost all strength as my eyes fell upon the room – it was simple, exquisite, without fuss. Stone floors, vaulted timber ceilings and Zen-style bed opened out onto a small private courtyard and an outside shower. The ground was laid with stones of every shape and size – large shiny ones, interspersed with small flint like pebbles. Aesthetically positioned plants made a perfect foil for the breathtaking view across lush curving hills ridged with rice terraces above the Petanu River. 'This is the life!' I thought.

Bali was a culture of many different worlds. It was so far from anything I'd previously known. The heat. The humidity. The people. All were so unfamiliar to my teenage experience in conservative, pinned up England. It was deeply exciting to be there, forging a path of my own in the world. But what I loved most were the Balinese people. They were unbelievable friendly, warm and accommodating, generous in their time and their hospitality. This, too, I'd never experienced. Despite the – to my mind – uncanny myths, beliefs and rituals, I would liked to have spent more time with the older Balinese – I found myself particularly drawn to their crinkled faces, cataracts, lopsided grins and crooked, tobacco stained teeth. It seemed their faces might tell a story I desperately wanted to hear.

With days running out till I was due in Melbourne, I was determined to explore the city while I could. Ubud's cooler temperature encouraged me to reconnoitre on foot. I felt very safe amongst the street's chaos – which in retrospect was a mistake. Jammed with traffic, I attempted to cross where three main roads intersected when a scooter, out of nowhere, clipped my heel and sent me flying.

It was the strangest experience – although I could see a few bystanders watching from a distance, no one stepped forward to help. And suddenly, I was eleven years old again. One summer I had smashed my teeth in the swimming pool, where my brothers and I had a season ticket for the school holidays. I turned cold inside thinking about my bloody face and broken teeth as I climbed the stairs to the neighbour's house where Mum was having tea and cake. A bright red nerve was sticking out from my severed tooth and a rather large piece was missing from another as I stood clasping bloody gauze to my chin.

"Go home. I'll be there shortly," Mum had said dismissively. I'd disturbed her treat.

"But she's as white as a ghost!" The neighbour said.

"She'll be fine," I heard Mum reply as I turned away to do as I was told.

I felt similarly stupid on that Ubud street. As I brushed the grit from my grazed palms and knees I berated myself for expecting someone to offer a helping hand. So, dragging myself up, I limped on mentally telling myself to suck it up and be a big girl. For a while I tried walking like a local – head up, eyes forward – trying to look as if I belonged there. I soon gave up – my ankles had had enough twisting for one day. I headed slowly back to the hotel, keeping my eyes peeled to the ground and reflecting that there was no point pretending to be a local or anything I wasn't – I'd only trip myself up.

I'd wanted to see the authentic Ubud – but it proved impossible to find. I particularly wanted to hear a full Gamalan in action, a traditional Indonesian instrumental ensemble comprising mainly percussion: gongs, xylophones, drums, cymbals and flutes. Unfortunately the experience escaped me; I had to stick with the memory of the partial Gamalan I'd once heard at a concert in the St Albans Town Hall at home. The Pura Taman Saraswati, with its water back-dropped stage enhancing the stunning display of costumes, dance and story telling, was thoroughly entertaining, as was the Barong dance I caught by accident, which tells of the never-ending battle between good and evil. It reminded me, though, of the boy I'd run away from. I knew he wasn't evil. I just didn't get why he'd hit me. I didn't deserve it. We'd had a good thing going I'd thought. Was I just in the wrong place at the wrong time when he suddenly felt frustrated? Young as I was, I struggled to understand. It was like it had happened to someone else. When the group began performing a traditional Tek Tok dance accompanied by musical 'tek tok' sounds made with the flicking of their tongues, the sound wove its way into my head, until it came to resemble the rhythm of the cuckoo clock that hung on the wall in my grandparent's hall. Backwards and forwards the tek tok reverberated, like a never-ending dance of apologies and fists that marked the movement of time. When it suddenly stopped, it was like coming out of a dream. Startled from my reverie, I instinctively knew I'd been lucky to escape, lucky to have the opportunity to run away. So many didn't have that chance. In the

silent moments after the dancing stopped, I vowed to myself that
– from that moment on – I'd never stand such nonsense from a
man again.

Later, I laughed out loud to hear there was a moral message
behind the tek tok dance. When a woman who embodied
patience, sacrifice, compassion, devotion and a holy sincerity
wasn't respected, disaster and calamity would befall the
Kingdom. Truth, virtue, devotion and genuine compassion, says
the story, will always be protected by God.

=><=

In my last few days I was determined to see more of the
countryside. I joined an amazing off-the-beaten-track cycle tour,
starting early with breakfast overlooking Mount Batur before
downhill cycling through jungle, rice paddies and villages deep
into rural Bali. And finally here was the authentic daily life of
local people — their age-old customs, back breaking work, and
foot sore and finger breaking activities up coconut trees.

Unfortunately, I wished I'd checked the hire equipment
before setting off. My bike wasn't as freewheeling as I fancied I
was. It came to grinding a halt – the brake jammed, the chain
flew off and, on the wobble, I joined it. The rice paddy emptied
– a dozen people came rushing to my aid. I had no idea what
they were yelling, but I waved with a smile. I stood up, brushed
myself off and rubbed my back. I noticed a couple of the 'old
buggers' bent in half rubbed their backs in tandem with me. I
couldn't figure if they were taking the rise, or whether their work
had got the better of them. Nevertheless, where the city folk had
offered no help, back broken farmers came running without
hesitation. I thanked them with a smile and a laugh – knowing
there was no chance we could understand each other – and began
the slow walk pushing the unwieldy bike back up hill.

The next day I tried my luck again at sightseeing without

incident. I engaged a driver to take me to the Sacred Monkey Forest. His name was Wyan, and he was an accommodating chappie like most of the Balinese people I'd met. Tall, dark and handsome with a delicate, almost feminine smile, he was both gentle and graceful, with long elegant limbs of lustrous tanned skin, toned and muscular. It seemed as if all the Indonesians I'd seen so far had all been either stunningly beautiful youths or leathery, wizened elders – there seemed to be no stage in between. Beyond his physical appearance, though, there was also something very attractive about Wyan – his relaxed, humorous nature, that glint in his eyes. To my seventeen year old self he was a Balinese Adonis.

"You have to risk losing something," he laughed when I told him I wanted to haggle with the monkeys. "You can't haggle for nothing. They like spectacles."

"Will I get them back?" I questioned. I didn't carry spares and I'd be lost without them.

"Depends how good a haggler you are," I heard him say as my specs were whipped off my head. In a flash, a monkey had swooped in and grabbed them. As it mocked me from an adjacent branch it seemed to be telling me to keep an eye out for potential thieves when I was on the road – and remember they can come in all shapes and sizes.

"What do I do?" I asked Wyan beseechingly. What followed was a crash course in the art of the haggle – a skill that would one day stand me in good stead when it came to negotiating corporate contracts.

Thankfully, Wyan was a good teacher. After he'd watched me chase the monkey up and down for a few minutes, both of us becoming quite irate, Wyan passed me a tangerine and told me to peel it.

Unsure, I did so, gently but firmly holding a few segments between forefinger and thumb and warily extending my arm. The monkey was clever – he'd played this game before. He put me at ease, approaching me as I had him – slowly and vigilantly. I fed him the tangerine segments. He decided to keep my glasses.

Next round, I proffered the tangerine to him with one hand while reaching for the monkey to hand over my glasses with the other. He grabbed the fruit snack and retreated quickly to a tree stump nearby, shaking his head at me as if to say, "Humans. So stupid."

"Try again," Wyan laughed, taking the tangerine. "Hold both hands flat, like this." I did exactly as he said.

"No. Flatter – push the centre of your palms up, fingertips down. Like a bridge," he instructed. "Yes! Perfect." He placed the last segments on my palm.

"Now, show the monkey both palms," he instructed.

I did exactly as I was told. I'm sure that monkey grinned.

"Please, please, don't break them," I begged, as Monkey placed my glasses on the tree stump beside him. Watchfully, he took the last of my tangerine – blew me a kiss and swung back up into the trees.

"First, you give and then you take!" said my teacher.

Duped! "That's not give and take!" I yelled.

"Isn't it?" he winked.

"You're a crook!" I yelled at Monkey, as Wyan laughed out loud.

Later, in the village of Petulu just outside Ubud I watched as 20,000 white and rusty orange coloured birds, Kokokan's (White Heron) tussled for a roosting spot. They'd been coming every evening since 1965, during the Communist massacres. A deep solemn feeling came over me.

"Wyan," I called. "I can't shake the feeling something very bad happened here." He joined me to gaze at the birds.

"According to the locals, these are the souls of the slaughtered, coming to visit their loved ones every night and leaving every dawn en masse," he told me, squeezing my shoulder.

That night, in my beachfront room, I was unable to ditch the souls of Petulu. I took a stroll along black sand near the water's edge, wondering why it had affected me so. I suddenly recalled the Ouija board my brothers and I used to play with… until the day mum actually made it work one, cold, wet British winter evening.

Mum was preparing dinner, listening through the serving hatch to our every word.

"What are you up to?" she called, when we'd fallen silent.

"Nothing," my eldest brother replied.

"I've got eyes in the back of my head!" she said, coming into the room and spying the Ouija board. "I've told you before, not to play with that!"

My brother kicked me under the table, prompting me to ask, "Why not? It's ours."

"Because! I said so!" she said. It was always the same. Never an explanation, just her stock standard response. This time was different though. This time, she placed the Ouija board in the centre of the table with our three small pairs of fingertips just touching the edge to hold the board in place. Then Mum, her fingers and thumbs curled into her palms, gently rested two long skinny fingers on the yellow plastic disk that looked like a big flat spinning top.

Six wide eyes focused on her intently.

"What are you going to ask, Mum?" I breathed.

"What would you like to know?" she questioned. I wanted to know if my dad would be home for Christmas.

Mum opened her mouth to ask the question. The disc turned quickly to 'yes' before it zapped, uncontrollably, from the table and hit the door.

"You're a witch. The both of you – bloody witches!" my

brother had cried. He'd got a swift smack for his language but the moment had stayed with me.

I'd had a fascination with the unexplained from the age of twelve when I ordered my first books from the school book club – 'Monsters of the Deep' and 'The Unexplained'. Then, when I was around fifteen, my mother suggested I visit a psychic. I don't quite remember why – had I been unsettled? Or was she just sick of my persistent questions?

I arrived at the large two storey Victorian house in Avenue Road (the name always amused me – couldn't someone make their mind up?). A petite woman with the blackest hair and the whitest face I'd ever seen opened the high front door. She'd added thick black-rimmed eyes to match her deep red lipstick. Softly spoken, she ushered me to a stool in the kitchen, placed to face her. She introduced herself, then her Spirit Guide, explaining apropos of nothing that she'd been poisoned numerous times (in this lifetime) and survived. She also claimed to have been Cleopatra – and I squirmed. Why can't psychics ever be normal, run of the mill people in the past? I wondered.

In an instant, the mood of the room changed. A formidable man's voice boomed from the fragile stick of a woman before me. I wasn't scared – I thought she was just being theatrical. Then her face changed from an old lady to a white haired man.

I nearly leapt off my stool. What had he said? I screwed up my face trying to focus in – where in the hell was the woman? An American Indian appeared to be sitting before me now, except his skin looked grey, like a pencilled sketch, and deeply crevassed. His hair was a silk white, wavy mane. The eyes looking into mine were dark and austere, but strangely I no longer felt scared. Mentally, I invited him to speak again – I'd be so surprised the first time that I'd missed what he'd said. But he'd already vanished, leaving behind in me a strong sense of familiarity and then sadness.

The memory had got me thinking. I'd once heard souls stuck

in limbo sometimes attached themselves to the living. I'd just ditched responsibility for my mum and sister by running away to Australia. Maybe I'd adopted the Petulu souls to replace them? It was the kind of thing I was prone to – adopting lost souls. I was always sticking up for the underdogs, but now I wondered why. Was I an underdog who just didn't know how to ask for help?

=><=

I'd invited Wyan to dine with me. I didn't know it then, but travelling alone carries a subconscious desire to make each personal connection count, however brief. Intense adventures and strong emotions made everything seem brighter, more acute.

"Thank you. But, I don't mix business with pleasure," he'd replied, in the nicest of tones.

"Oh. I'm sorry. I hope I didn't offend you?" I said, "I didn't want you dining alone." I had no ulterior motive. Inviting a lone individual, or offering a traveller a drink is something I'd learned as a kid, from my sociable, magnanimous father. It had become a habit, and I wanted to prolong the wonderful day we'd had.

Deep in thought, I dined by myself poolside while he took his meal and rest on a thatch-roofed platform nearby — I mentally wished him luck with the night bugs.

"Do you have Kokokan on the menu?" I asked the waiter who came to get my order. It sounds gruesome (and my only defence for suggesting I dine on his sacred bird was I was still a kid) but I'd been thinking to put the souls – and myself – to rest by eating them. I'd had a notion it might send them on their way with good tidings. The waiter awkwardly recommended the Babi Guling instead, which turned out to be quite the culinary experience – spit-roast pig served with rice and spiced veggies, offal and black pudding. Afterwards, I slept like the dead all night.

From Ubud, Wyan and I did a whistle-stop tour the length of the country through perfectly layered terraces of rice paddies or cabbage, maize and potato plantations to the northern coast at Lovina, famed for its beauty and serenity. Though I tried valiantly, I knew seeing everything would be impossible. I'd have to return here someday. On my final day, we hit the road for a quick morning dip at the Banjar Hot Spring, arriving early to avoid the crowds. I tried all three pools, then joined Wyan who had been waiting patiently under the spouts that delivered a wonderfully intense water massage to our backs and shoulders — bliss! Invigorated yet relaxed, we wandered back to Singaraja – once the Island's capital – where I'd forgotten myself and unconsciously reached for Wyan's hand. In the nick of time, a thankful jolt brought me back to reality and we parted ways amicably.

I explored one last temple and took in an array of artefacts at the Gedong Kirtya Lontar Museum, including fourteenth century royal decrees, calendars and an amazing palm leaf collection of books, seals, historical narratives and, surprisingly, future predictions. Gazing on them behind tempered glass, I wondered at my own future. Had I escaped my problems? What was left to me in the UK – a bashing boyfriend, a family that didn't care?

"Do you believe we can predict the future?" I asked the rickshaw driver on the way back to pick up my bags at the hotel. He was a funny little man. He reminded me of Yoda. His small round head, big eyes, milky grey surrounded with bright whites and 'long wispy, white beard. His shrivelled skin had a soft hue and plenty of lines. His appearance and demeanour suggested he had lived long and well.

The driver paused for a long time, with a look in his eye that said he knew exactly what I'd asked.

"The future is the future. It'll be – no matter what," he said, cryptically.

From my hotel balcony I gazed out for the last time over

almost luminous rice terraces. Bali had touched my soul. Moreover, it had awakened me. I felt like I'd been spiritually cleansed. The island of the Gods had taught me to be proud, stand tall and be a leader not a follower. I would live my life my way, for me and nobody else. I'd learned to be me, no matter what.

===><===

4
AUSTRALIA

I was so excited to see my grandparents. Whisked to their home in Belgrave Heights at the foothills of the Dandenong Ranges, I was fed and watered on the deck as I overlooked the gully where my grandfather fed kookaburras with, to my surprise, kangaroo meat.

I could see my grandfather had something on his mind, so I created a pause — I wished I hadn't.

"I just don't understand why people put up with violent partners," he said, with a disapproving tone, as though I were the perpetrator not the victim. I tried not to cry as I confirmed the story my mother had, to my dismay, already told him. I was pretty ticked off with her. I usually never talked anything through with my parents, or anyone else, come to think of it – whether it was good news, bad or indifferent. I didn't want to burden them. In this I was much like my grandfather, who used to mutter, "That's my business," if someone asked too many questions. Like him, I wanted to choose what to tell when – that way I could be prepared.

Granddad listened to my story but thankfully refrained from

any more judgement, simply patting me on the shoulder. And that was the last time we spoke of the matter.

For three consecutive days, my grandparents drove me all over the Ranges – they loved a road trip. Unfortunately for my seventeen-year-old self, they weren't so keen on getting out of the car. The back of their dear grey-haired heads framed much of what I saw and, as much as I loved them, for a teenager it was akin to touristic torture.

One exception was a place called William Rickets Sanctuary. Rickets had carved indigenous figures into the trees in a naturally beautiful and tranquil woodland setting. His message in doing so was to suggest, all of us are custodians of our natural environment as the indigenous peoples had been – and still are. Half-hidden among huge ferns so tall and wide they resembled umbrellas, I felt the eyes of his mystical sculptures watching my every step. As we meandered the winding pathways of the four-acre bush block, I realised their gaze felt normal to me. In fact, I'd always felt like I was being watched, even as a young child, as if I was expected to do something. At the sanctuary, the feeling was simply stronger – as if invisible keepers of the Earth were intently watching my every move. I had the distinct impression they were telling me to do no wrong as I walked the paths.

It was the first time such an impression had a strong indelible effect on me, but it wasn't to be the last. I'd never bought into the whole notion of God, but I did feel there were natural forces far greater than we understand. For me the Earth's Keepers (as I came to call them) were like imaginary friends. Throughout the years I'd ask them to help me make wiser choices or keep me safe during my travels. I wasn't so touched as to think they were real, but they served a symbolic purpose, I guess. They kept me on the straight and narrow when my natural tendency to flout authority kicked in. When I insisted on governing my own destiny without interference from others, the Earth's Keepers would be my judges and jury. No one else could tell me what to do.

It was lovely spending time with my grandparents but a teenager can only take so many giant ferns, mountain ash and 300 foot eucalypts before she starts getting twitchy. In the back seat of my Granddad's Outback I stopped looking at the scenery and began mentally planning my next adventure.

Walkabout

Australia's interior is largely miles of nothingness — scrub-filled, arid landscapes reaching to the edge of the horizon that makes you understand why people once thought the earth was flat. I stayed with my grandparents and worked for a while in Melbourne so I could afford to go backpacking across the continent. Though it wasn't so long ago, in 1982 the world seemed so much bigger. No flash-packers, just the odd town comprising a filling station, bar (if you were lucky), and a public phone that rarely worked. Occasionally you'd meet fellow travellers heading in the opposite direction and have an opportunity to chat — some tourists, some locals, some natives. Without mobile devices, good old-fashioned conversation promoted an exchange of information about upcoming towns, accommodation, and things to do and not do. It was thrilling to speak to travellers who'd just done what you were about to. Hearing and feeling their excitement or disappointment was enough to help you make decisions or change your plans, if you had any.

I'd taken a Greyhound bus north from Adelaide through South Australia and along the Stuart Highway toward Alice Springs. Over hundreds of kilometres up through Port Pirie and Port Augusta across deserts and miles of scrub, I gazed out of the dusty window thinking about those who'd helped fuel my great escape. There was my mother who'd initiated the trip and my brother who'd paid me to prepare his tax return – a task I normally did for free. I could even thank my crazy ex-boyfriend – not that I felt thankful for being bashed and bruised! Yet, but for those awful circumstances, I'd never have learned to be vigilant and how to keep my possessions and myself safe (especially when hanging out with cheeky monkeys). I'd begun to understand why it was so important to have self-respect, be positive about life and stay strong despite adversity. As Robert H. Schuller said, "Tough times never last. But tough people do."

Most of all I learned gratitude.

As I travelled through the opal-mining town, Coober Pedy, which, 150 million years ago, had been covered by a vast inland ocean and was now almost completely built underground, I felt as if I'd been reborn. I had a clean slate – a chance to learn how to be truly 'me.' Past Mount Connor, a big flat-topped mountain also known as Attila to the domed Kata Tjuta (The Olgas), and on to Uluru (then it was called Ayres Rock), I prepared for a new beginning, a new me. It was like I'd glimpsed real freedom for the first time in my life.

My room for the night was an isolated wooden shack miles from anywhere. The shower water, what there was of it, had been warmed by the desert sun and tinted pink from the fine red sand that somehow seeped into everything; the contents of my backpack had turned red in the bus' hold. Cleaned up and ready to join a twilight tour, I travelled to a lookout to watch the sun set over Uluru. Cameras set to snap at thirty-second intervals, I waited with a handful of tourists for the sun to start its descent, changing the colour of The Rock from dark red to bright orange and lighting up the clouds in swathes of pinks, purples and the most magnificent, heart-wrenching blues I'd ever seen. As the sun dropped behind Uluru the sky burst into flame coloured beauty, as if it were some kind of enormous altar built to worship a sun god. Suddenly sun cults made perfect sense – how could you not believe in the face of so much majesty. It was hypnotic. My heart filled with wonder.

That night I could barely sleep. I wanted to see more. At four in the morning, I quietly packed up and departed, leaving my backpack with a note attached to it at the end of my roommate, Lucy's bed, asking her to put it on the bus for me. Under a clear sky of sparkling desert stars, I walked for an hour through the scrub towards the huge rock in the distance. I'd learned the day before that it once sat at the bottom of an ocean. Now only a sixth of it sits above ground; the remaining two and a half kilometres hides beneath the soil.

Eventually I reached a trail, well worn in parts and virtually non-existent in others. The isolation was satisfyingly eerie, particularly because the case of little Azaria Chamberlain, who at six months old had been taken from her tent and killed, was big news at that time. Her mother, Lindy, had been jailed for murder and later released when, by chance, Azaria's matinee jacket had been found in a dingo's lair at the base of Uluru. You'd think that would be the end of the matter – in fact it would take thirty-two years and four inquests to conclude that a dingo had killed her baby.

I trekked past caves of ancient paintings and cordoned off areas marked 'sacred', 'man' or 'woman'. It took me three hours to walk Uluru's base in the pale morning light, with occasional stops to relish the atmosphere and appreciate rock formations. As the first tour bus of the day pulled in, I watched as a stick-thin old man leaped out, dragging his equally stick-thin wife towards the climb. It seemed funny at first, cartoon-like, but then I'd feared for them, as she was clearly not as keen to climb as he. The wind was forceful, whipping away sun hats, caps and anything that wasn't firmly secured to the climbers. The climb was slow and dangerous beyond the chain — I didn't stick around to see if they'd made it.

I can still feel the joy of getting off the bus at Three Ways, where I spotted a girl I'd met en route from Melbourne to Adelaide in the roadhouse. I was on top of the world — free and about to celebrate my eighteenth birthday; now I had someone to celebrate with on my way to Alice Springs. Monica was a power tower – just short of six feet, with a brunette cascade of dead straight, shiny hair and striking, almost masculine, features. She looked like she had Red Indian blood coursing through her veins. Her haunting hazel – almost golden – eyes were unlike any I'd seen. We'd explored Adelaide together but parted ways when I continued on to the Northern Territory. We knew each other's general travel plans but things change when you're on the road. You go as the wind blows, or where the sun shines.

"So, did you meet with your friends, as planned?" I asked.

"I did, but we didn't have much time. They finished their exams, then shipped out," she said, "But I crossed paths with Blue Eyes."

Dougal was adorable. I can't say it was love at first sight; but maybe second! Those eyes and that sensational Glaswegian accent made me melt. Broad and soft, his rolling 'R's' drew me in. He was a smidge taller than me, definitely broader – apparently he'd been a karate champ though it was hard to believe with his half-inch thick lenses. I felt a little jealous Monica had got to hang out with him again, just as the three of us had.

"Do you remember that first night?" I asked.

"Oh yeah, the night he walked in?" she clarified. "Talk about six degrees of separation."

Just off the Greyhound from Melbourne, we'd been waiting outside an Adelaide youth hostel when up walked a couple of guys.

"I know them," Monica had nudged me.

"Sure you do," I murmured, disinterested. I'd already made it clear I wasn't on the pull – I was done with blokes for a while.

Turned out she did know them. They'd crossed paths somewhere in South America a few months before.

"It's a small world," Monica called to the guys.

"And, you never know who you'll meet," Dougal retorted.

Neither of us realised then how prescient that statement would prove to be.

=><=

My eighteenth birthday in Alice Springs was one of my most memorable. There wasn't much to the town except a dry riverbed, a telegraph station a long hike out of town and a Kentucky Fried Chicken — but not a golden arch yet in sight; McDonalds was yet to blight landscapes so far afield from the US and Europe.

"I want to do something special for my birthday," I said to the tour agent. "How about a safari?"

Rather than the lions, tigers, and giraffes the word immediately conjures, my birthday safari was more about puddles of water, rocks, trees and a few wallabies. Six of us (including the driver) headed off the beaten track in a well-used four-wheel drive. I was surprised to discover the desert was very much alive, and so was I. I'd never seen such depth of colour in nature before. I was mesmerised. The day delivered one wonder after another — eucalypts growing out of sheer rock, seemingly without water. Towering sandstone, rich in iron, presented luscious ochre walls perfectly contrasted to the unexpected pristine clear blue water pooled under the burning desert heat and the infamously blue Australian sky. Lush greenery sprouted randomly amongst the vast, arid nothingness. And then, as the day ended, came the best surprise of all.

"Hey, birthday girl!" The voice seemed to drift on the night air. Who in the middle of nowhere knew it was my birthday? Only Monica, who was walking beside me.

"Who's there?" I called into the dark.

"Come and see. We're celebrating," came the reply in a soft Scottish brogue.

Like planned synchronicity, Monica and I looked at each and, without a word, changed direction towards where we could hear laughing and cracking ring pulls. Before my eyes could adjust to the light, I was encased in a huge bear hug.

"Oh, my god! What are you doing here?" I exclaimed. I wasn't sure whether I should hug Blue Eyes, or Monica.

"Did you know? Did you tell him?" I said, to Monica, with the broadest grin and widest eyes. I spent the entire night barbequing, telling tales around the campfire, joking and generally clowning around with Dougal, Monica and his travelling buddies. Away from pollution, under a star-filled sky in the middle of nowhere, it was a perfect birthday, never to be forgotten.

=><=

My long circuitous road trip had me back in Melbourne just as Australia Day was approaching and Monica's friend had issued a camping invitation to celebrate the long weekend. I had yet to reply; I was feeling unable to commit. Nevertheless, I accompanied Monica to the camping store in search of a blow up mattress, equipment, and a pair of walking boots for me. As I crouched on the floor, rummaging for my size, another pair of feet drew alongside us.

"So, are you coming or not?" a brash male voice asked. As I raised my eyes, with thoughts of 'who the heck are you?' I realised the question had been directed at me.

"I don't know, I haven't decided yet," I replied, feeling irked that this stranger was pushing me to make a decision. I had a feeling he'd wanted to be more than just friends with Monica, and I'd probably be in the way. I wasn't sure he'd really want a fly in the ointment, there would be enough little black buggers buzzing around, anyway – t'was the season.

"That means 'no' then!" Came the rejoinder. Confused, I pulled my head back, with an involuntary frown.

"No, it doesn't. It means I haven't decided," and I returned to rummaging.

Monica, in airhead mode, drove the large four-wheel drive into a pillar as she reversed. She was clearly distracted, consumed by her brief encounter. I don't know how many times I heard her say, to my annoyance, that she was surprised to see her friend in the camping outlet store when he was just passing through. So what? Had I missed something? I was feeling peeved and just wanted to be alone for a while – as sometimes happens when you're travelling with others.

The next morning I had a message at the front desk:

If you're coming & you want to travel with Dougal, call him to make arrangements.

Well, that changed things! I got packing.

=><=

Mid-morning a black jeep rolled down the side of the block and drew to a stop by me.

Is that all you're going to take?" Dougal called cheerfully.

"Yep," I proudly smiled, fixing the small red pack on my shoulder and stooping for the carrier bag of provisions.

"Okay. Load 'er up," he laughed, shaking his head. Jumping into the passenger seat, I was amazed to see a Big Ugly Mutt – a stubbed tailed boxer, amongst the provisions neatly stacked almost to the roof.

"Don't worry about Flashy, he won't bite," Dougal grinned. "He's a superstar dog! I'm looking after him for a friend."

Flashy promptly clambered all over me and squeezed himself into a tight ball in the floor well by my feet as we pulled out on the highway. The three-hour road trip flew by. We got along like a house on fire – chatting away as if we'd known each other forever.

"Wait till you see where we're going – it's a fine place to camp!" Dougal enthused.

Feeling the need to come clean, I stared ahead for a while.

"I don't like camping," I muttered, half hoping he wouldn't hear.

"What! You don't like camping?" Dougal, laughed. "What are you doing here then?"

"Well, sunny Jim – it sure ain't the camping," I replied, looking at him with a cheeky smile.

"Have you ever been?" He asked.

I explained that on two previous occasions I'd camped with so-called camping kings. Both times were a complete disaster – the first, we ended up drying everything in a local launderette. And the second – well, let's just call it a bad choice of companion.

"Ah, ma wee wild child, this time'll be different," he said, confidently.

"How so?" I asked, daring him to dazzle me.

"Let's see," he replied, "How about, a front row seat to the most beautiful, serene and tranquil spot on the river. In the moonlight, under a star-studded sky, you'll be wined, dined and entertained by an open fire. Then, snuggled together, you'll think you're floating on a cloud." He darted a quick look over at me.

If you like?" He added, a little sheepishly.

"If only!" I chuckled.

We stopped in a small town for last minute provisions, including a bag or two of ice.

"Hey, why don't we pitch somewhere here for a night? We can meet up with Monica and her mate tomorrow – or the day after?" he asked. "They might appreciate some alone time. How about you?"

"Sound's good to me," I grinned, a bit starry eyed.

A few kilometres out we turned off onto the unmade side road and then into the forested area to the river, where we crossed the rickety bridge to the island known as Dick's Bend.

It was absolutely divine — the gum trees' aroma, the silence of the bush (except for the odd bird twitters). While the mad mutt bounded on all fours and launched himself into the river, we unloaded the car. I laughed, chuckled and poked as much fun as I could get away with — I couldn't believe the amount of stuff to unload! Not a plastic cup or plate to be seen, all fine glass.

"This isn't camping!" Called I, the ignorant.

"It is where I come from," Dougal assured me, making a dashing figure while pitching the tents.

If heaven existed, here was the evidence. The Mighty River Murray supports fauna, flora and local communities along its 2,500 kilometre length, was warm and refreshing as we sought to escape the heat. The soft, sparkling water floated past; full of minerals it caressed our bodies, as did our hands. We were in heaven - lost in time and space. There was nothing else that mattered, as we frolicked, naked, in the waters between the dry encrusted banks. Around us 300-foot gum trees shimmered, reflecting an incredible light I've only ever known under the Australian sky.

"Look at the colour of that sky, "I said, skimming the water skyward. "Now, that's blue!"

"Indeed, it is. None of your wishy-washy stuff," Dougal replied. "And not a cloud in sight."

"Yep, none of your British rubbish," I retorted, diving to pull his legs out from him.

"I'm so pleased you agreed to stop," Dougal said, after he'd come up spluttering and chased me around the river for a while. "We couldn't be so free with Monica and her mate around."

As I was about to respond, my new four-legged friend

launched himself from the bank, dividing us in a spray of water and setting us laughing all over again.

$$= > < =$$

From a billabong rug by the water I watched Dougal the campfire king start dinner — I offered help, but there was nothing doing. Fun, challenging conversation and general 'bloke-ish' clowning around — this was the perfect preamble to a lasting friendship. He told me about his parents, his grannie and his travels. He waxed lyrical about the Yucatan, the Maya and their ruins, the Tzompantli, the wall of skulls — where the heads of sacrificial victims were placed on racks. And his eyes glowed as he discussed the giant ball court, where losing teams lost their heads. Hilarity prevailed as we chose our fantasy sacrificial teams, deciding which of our friends we'd offer to the Gods first.

"Gin and tonic? Ice and lemon?" He asked, heading to the Eskie.

As we warmed ourselves by the fire, I told him about my peripatetic life, how my parents moved me around, and how I came to be in Australia.

"Ah! You poor thing," he said, drawing me tight into his side. "Never mind, you've got me now. I'll be your Prince Charming and look out for you if you wish?"

"I prefer my men tall, dark and handsome," I teased.

"Counts me out, then?" he shrugged, giving me a 'no chance' look.

"Absolutely… not," I fired back.

"Would you care to take your seat then, sweet pea? Dinner is served," Dougal intoned, folding a charred tea towel neatly over his forearm.

For starters we feasted on thinly sliced, lime-cured salmon with a smattering of French mustard and dill, with warm bread on the side. Then it was a whole baby barramundi to share, garnished with lemon slices and small, fire baked potatoes, topped with lemon infused butter. There was also a fresh, garden salad in a bowl for helping yourself.

"Red or White?" he asked, presenting the labels.

"You've done this before," I said amazed at what I saw before me – it seemed better than any restaurant I'd been to.

"I promise you're the first and last," he said with a sly wink, but I didn't believe him. The way he brandished the dishes for my delectation was too practiced. But what did I care? As holiday romances went, it was pretty perfect.

As he laid out a selection of cheeses on a beautiful olive wood board and topped up my glass, he spoke avidly about his great loves – food, wine and travel. I couldn't help but concur – I'd only seen a little of the world so far, but I'd definitely caught the bug. There was so much to explore I never wanted to stop. I relished the feeling of freedom too much.

Yet as darkness fell and the mesmeric, deep orange flames flicked the breeze, I suddenly also felt deeply connected to this man in a way I'd never felt before. Unlike my ex, here was someone who, first and foremost, would keep his fists to himself – even though he seemed as if he could handle himself in a fight. And I truly believed he'd meant what he said about being there for me.

Later Dougal, Flashy and I lay side by side on a tartan billabong rug as I traced my fingers along the scars on his face.

"What's this one?" I whispered.

"A boy from the big school chased me up the road with a hammer," he remembered. "I was too slow. But I put up a good fight." He moved my fingers to his nose.

"This got crooked during a championship point. Crystal palace," he laughed drawing my finger down its ridge, "That was a tough fight. They were hard times."

"Mid-winter, no-matter the weather, the coaches had us run

barefoot around the track, virtually naked, just shorts," he continued. "They'd hose us with ice cold water as we passed."

I listened intently, hanging on every word. Though I hadn't known him long, I felt like he was a kindred soul.

"If you're going to marry, marry your best friend," my grandmother once told me. Was I meeting my best friend right now? I wasn't prepared for a meaningful relationship – but I already knew timing rarely worked on one's own terms. I felt a little nervous. I wasn't sure I was ready. To cover my apprehension, I jumped up.

"I hereby proclaim Dick's Bend is my place and camping is now my thing!" I decried, holding my wine glass aloft.

"Kim of the Forest, I dub thee," Dougal laughed lifting an imaginary sword from my shoulder.

We fell back to earth, laughing and staring into each other's eyes. Yep, I was caught. Hook, line and sinker.

===><===

5
SCOTLAND

Five days after Dougal and I spent that magical long weekend at Dick's Bend, he returned home to Glasgow.

Heartbroken but philosophical, I moved on relatively quickly, as teenagers can. It was the way of holiday romances and we'd made noises about meeting up again if I was ever in Scotland. Thing is, it took me a few years to get there.

=><=

I'd been working for a time in London for a financial services company when Beesie, a Scottish friend from Dumfries, called me with an offer.

"Hey, I've got tickets to the Edinburgh festival next week. Do you want to join me?" Beesie asked in her warm Scottish brogue. "I've got use of my boss' apartment for the week, so accommodation is free."

I jumped at the chance, thinking it the perfect opportunity to have a quick explore around Scotland while I was there. I'd meant to go many a time, even tried locating Dougal but by the time I'd returned from Australia he'd moved on from the address he'd given me.

Beesie welcomed me at the door of the apartment she'd secured. I was pleasantly surprised to see it was in The Vaults, one the oldest commercial buildings in Scotland. The charming historic sandstone building's air of nostalgia drew me in immediately – it had once housed the Scottish Malt Whisky Society beneath its stone steps. A Drambuie advertisement had been filmed there and it was a stone's throw from the Old Port of Leith, where gourmands flocked to eat by the waterside and amongst the narrow, bustling, character-filled streets. Once known as the Blak-Volts, it stood three stories above ground and a block below where two vaulted, seventy-foot cellars in an undercroft had been built in 1587. It wasn't a huge leap to imagine them connected to tunnels under Holyrood Palace, regularly ferrying the King's 'spirit' to and fro. But I would discover all this later.

Beesie had to get back to work, but promised we'd catch up on each other's latest news over a glass of wine later in the day. She wanted me to meet her at a local café for lunch, introduce me to the boss who had lent us the apartment and buy him a drink for his trouble.

After I'd unpacked and spent a goodly amount of time gazing out the apartment window at the forecourt below, which had an almost tangible atmosphere of hard toil etched into its cobbled pavements, I made my way to the café in Edinburgh proper.

I'd arrived a little early. The café was empty so I took a small table in the back corner and waited on the ornate, tapestry covered, wrap around seat as it progressively filled for lunch.

"Excuse me," said the waiter. "I have three gentlemen wanting to eat. It's a bit of a squeeze, but would you mind if they sat here?" He pointed to the empty chairs at my table.

"Not at all," I said, "But I'm waiting for two colleagues. We could put the two small tables together to seat six. If the gents don't mind?"

They were a lively trio and I soon became engrossed in conversation with them – they reminded me of Clegg, Compo and the Major, characters from Last of the Summer Wine. One – an Irishman – proudly explained how he'd lost his leg in a dynamite blast. Another, over six-foot, thin and straight, regaled me of stories of the Colonel's daughter he'd met as a boy soldier. I was just hearing the third man's story when they exploded in a cacophony of laughter and surprise – someone they knew had just unexpectedly appeared.

At the same time Beesie appeared by my side.

"I'm so sorry to keep you waiting," she said. "We were caught up with clients."

"Ladies, can I get you a drink?" called the man my three raucous tablemates had recognised from the bar.

I turned. Raised my eyebrows. Silence fell. The instant felt like eternity.

"You two know each other?" Beesie and the three men asked, astonished.

"Way longer than you can imagine," I replied. I couldn't stand up quick enough as he made his way to me.

"What are you doing here?" he asked incredulously, enveloping me in a hug.

"Waiting for you," I whispered.

=><=

It wasn't long before I'd ditched my London job and moved up to Glasgow to be closer to Dougal. He found me a job in his company – he said they could always use good financial experts and we both jumped at any excuse to see each other day and night.

It was like I'd known him forever – even though we had as

good as just met. It wasn't his rugged, swarthy good looks that caught my imagination – it was something in his eyes. I felt an overwhelming connection I'd never known, let alone understood. The feelings we shared were captivating but I wanted so much more. It felt like he might be my destiny, and I wanted to know if there was a future for us together.

Dougal even helped me find a place of my own – an elevated, ground floor flat in a red sandstone tenement with its Wally Close (tiled corridor) and unkempt front garden not much bigger than a window box.

"You have to live in a place to really know it, to get beneath its skin and let it get under yours," Dougal said. "If you stay here five years, it'll double in price."

"Five years!" I squirmed, "I've never stayed anywhere more than five months!"

"Well, now you have a reason to," he replied.

The interior was far from perfect but the location was superb — in the West End, next to the River Kelvin and within spitting distance of the Botanic Gardens through which I walked each morning to board the Clockwork Orange (the Underground) bound for my city office. It took a while, but I refurbished and reconfigured the rooms in my one bedroom abode, finally planting a beautiful pink fuchsia that quickly found its way along the picket fence – it was the first place I felt I could really call home. "Ma wee fla'."

Life was great. We took advantage of everything the Scottish cities, highlands and islands offered. Twenty-five years later, friends still tell me I go gooey when I talk about Dougal.

"You know, every time I mention his name, you're whole face lights up," a girl in my office once said.

They say couples shouldn't work together but we didn't care. After all, they also say those who play together, stay together. We worked hard and played harder. But Dougal saw the writing on the wall.

"You're wasted in this game," he said. "This financial service malarkey isn't going to survive the copious regulations coming up and as much as I love seeing you every day, you know you can do so much more."

I had to reluctantly agree. I'd taken the job primarily to be near Dougal and in truth I wasn't feeling very stretched. Although I was having a great time working alongside my eternally optimistic entrepreneur, I worried my lack of prospects in the role would eventually lead to boredom and ruin our relationship.

Still, there were benefits to being in each other's pockets. With clients all over, Dougal and I took every opportunity to explore the British roads usually less travelled, taking the opportunity to stay in hidden villages en-route. If we couldn't travel the world together at least we could find adventures in our backyard.

As we'd turn into yet another un-signposted lane, I'd be in stitches as Dougal called out: "Baton down the hatches and man the barricades! The Gerries are coming!" Removed during the WWII to confuse the Germans, many failed to reappear. Each time we'd roll the dice and hope we'd get to our destination (there were no Google maps back then). Privately I was proud to be by his side – he was smart, hilarious and full of fascinating titbits of information – at least to my twenty-something self. We both had a dry sense of humour that got us through every eventuality, but in retrospect we were rather childlike. We looked for the fun in everything.

One night, in the middle of nowhere, Dougal's run-flats ran flat. Dougal was desperate to return for a client meeting in the morning, so his phone was running hot calling the closest mechanics and finding us emergency accommodation.

"Three days to get the parts!" he exclaimed, pacing furiously by the side of the road. "No way! Twenty-four hours at most!"

As Dougal fumed, a tow truck drew alongside us.

"Hop in, I'll take you into town then come back for your motor," the driver called through the half open window. "Not a night for breaking down, is it? Got somewhere to stay?"

"We've managed to book a room at the Mason's Arms," I explained politely, glancing sideways at my still seething boyfriend.

"Nice! Best in the area, you know. Great history. Gets great reviews I hear," he replied.

It better be good, I thought to myself. Neither of us was in the mood for slumming it. It had been a long day and I didn't relish witnessing Dougal's humour if the parts didn't arrive pronto.

We pulled up in front of a traditional English village staging house, with wattle and daub walls and a thatched roof. A warm glow shone through square paned windows across boxes filled with bright flowers.

"I'll check in," I said, jumping out the truck quickly and giving Dougal space to clear his head. "I'll meet you in the bar when you're ready."

It wasn't long before he joined me.

"Sorry," he said sheepishly. "I think I've sorted parts for tomorrow."

"Perfect," I stretched to plant a comforting kiss on his cheek. "How about we order room service and retire for the evening?"

Later, I drew him a hot, bubbly bath as he nestled in a well-used antique bedroom chair with a double shot. At the risk of losing my hand, I took the glass from his hand and lured him over to the tub.

"Come on," I said softly, easing him from the chair. "A nice long soak should do the job."

Wrapped in big white, fluffy monogrammed goonies (dressing-gowns), we snuggled in under the abundantly feathered doona and settled into sleep as outside the night grew wild. Rain and wind lashed the windows while and a strange, persistent buzzing built to an interminable crescendo.

"What's that bloody noise?" I nudged a dozing Dougal with my elbow.

"No peace for the wicked, eh?" He grumbled in his rolling accent, flicking the switch and throwing back the doona.

Swarming above us was a brace of big ugly bluebottle type.

"Even Australian flies aren't that big," I cried, giggling.

"Grab your cork hat, love and help me with these wild beasties," he laughed, his passingly good attempt at an Aussie accent devolving into Weegie as he swatted at them.

Swat! Miss. Zap! Miss. Tears of laughter streamed down my face as I watched a naked Dougal launch himself around the room, like Mr Magoo.

Life with Dougal wasn't always so crazy. In our day jobs, we were the consummate professionals – diligent, forthright and competent to a fault. I thought Dougal was a super star. He, a generous lover, a fun companion and a great mentor and I really believed we were destined to be together for the rest of our lives.

$$=><=$$

It didn't take me long to find a Project Manager role that I was better suited to, but I did miss travelling the countryside with Dougal. Still, rarely a day would pass that we didn't meet before work to have egg and bacon or a square sausage in a delicious Scottish morning roll at the bakery on Exchange Square. Molten butter and bacon grease always went down well with a strong mug of coffee and news worthy conversation. I'd head around the corner, Dougal up the road, but not before a passionate kiss and long embrace to see us through the day.

"See you later," we'd say. "Love you."

On the odd occasion, lunch would turn into an afternoon session of debauchery in Squires, a popular bar for the business sorts. Sometimes, when we were really lost in each other's company, the lunchtime crowd would be replaced with the evening crew before we noticed. Once I'd stood at the end of the long narrow bar, watching Dougal holding court with a group of women. They seemed to be hanging on every word. For a second we locked eyes and smiled.

"Enjoy, girls," I thought to myself. "He's coming home with me." No animosity, no jealousy – I simply knew neither of us had room in our hearts for anyone else.

=><=

"Hey, I've got good news!" I exclaimed as I let myself into Dougal's apartment. "They want me to stay on as Programme Director of the integration."

My emotions were all over the place. I'd been hanging out for an opportunity to really prove myself. I'd enrolled with a professional body to extend my credentials, taken on extra subjects, studied hard, and passed everything. Dougal had supported me all the way, even going so far as to read my books so he could challenge me and help me deepen my knowledge. I felt more than ready to make my way up the illustrious corporate ladder.

"See. I said you were a wee superstar," he grinned. "Where shall we go to celebrate?"

"Well, I haven't agreed to take it yet. I'd like your thoughts, first," I said quietly. "I'll be based in Dublin, but not for long," I quickly added. "About six months, I'd guess."

"Ah! That's brilliant!" he replied, brimming with excitement, "I'll come over for weekends. And when you're done we'll tour around then take the overnight boat back to Glasgow together. It'll be just like the old days!"

Dublin

I worked out of a sumptuous family-owned hotel in quaint Malahide with a stunning view over the marina to distant grasslands and not an Irish accent in earshot. It was a festive season, truly one to remember. We laughed so hard, when we couldn't escape that driving rain.

Rugged up, Dougal, took my hand. "Come on," he said. "Let's check out the town. You can show me where you've been hanging out."

"We'll start down by the harbour," I said, pointing to the dinky coloured lights in the distance.

We walked cautiously, observing the settled snow in the corners of the abundantly decorated window displays. Shopkeepers stood in their doorways calling special offers and last minute, early bird bargains, trying to entice customers with mulled wine and other festive niceties. Everyone's spirits were high as they went about their business in the beautiful festive, village atmosphere.

"Ahh!" I shrieked, tightening my grip on Dougal's hand. I'd slipped on the ice, concealed by the fresh laid snow. I'd nearly pulled him down with me but fortunately he dug in and softened my landing. With the greatest of care and concern, he helped me to my feet.

"Ooh, be careful." He asked, "Are you hurt?" I'd twisted my ankle and skinned my chin. I'd been quite clumsy recently for some reason and I was black and blue as a result.

"Only you would fall in front of a bar," he mocked, pointing up to a sign that read "Special Mulled Wine."

"What's a girl's got to do for a drink?" I groaned, making a face.

"C'mon, ma lady," he teased, bowing like a consort. "Let's get you a winter warmer." He helped me inside, making sure I didn't slip again.

Nestled in the corner by the fire, we warmed our insides with a delicious mulled brew, managing to catch up on each other's news since we'd last met despite the jigging and foot tapping to the local band going on around us.

For me, there was little better than settling with my love, snuggled side by side, completely absorbed in conversation. We'd listen intently to each other's tales, subconsciously picking up on key details and nuances. We could read each other perfectly.

Unfortunately, Dougal hadn't been able to visit as often as we would have liked – work had been punishing. When he did we spent our weekends trawling bars in search of live music and the legendary Irish craic, despite Dougal's virulent attacks of gout and my unsteadiness of step. It was a wonderful time and it helped my stay in Dublin fly by.

Soon the contract was satisfied and Dougal arrived for our departing tour.

It was late. "How about dinner at Aniar?" Dougal said with a mischievous glint in his eyes.

Aniar is the only Michelin starred restaurant in Galway that's adopted old traditional cooking and preservation methods, such as curing, pickling and fermenting to enhance the orgasmic delights of their wild contemporary Irish offerings of locally produced ingredients.

It was a long drive and I doubted we'd get a table without a reservation, but – hell – I was up for a road trip if he was.

"We'd better get a wiggle on if we're to make last orders," I said, grabbing my coat.

Slavering over the menu, we enjoyed an 'amuse bouche' of deep fried pigskin with duck parfait inside, sprinkled with a vinegar powder.

"Mmm, delicious. I do like a good bit of pork crackling," Dougal said.

"Here, have mine. I'm not so keen on the vinegar flavour," I said reaching across the table. He stretched his head forward to clasp my offering between his teeth.

"Not my fingers!" I yelped whipping away my hand.

"A traitor to your roots!" he claimed. "You're no Lithuanian! Aren't vinegars and pickles supposed to be your national dish?"

Starters arrived. Scallops, oyster, dillisk, wood sorrel, and smoked potato. My eyes glued and my innards collapsed in satisfaction, feeling Dougal's pleasure as he slowly drew air passed his lips.

"Hmmm," he uttered. "The smokiness in this emulsion is cooked to perfection."

"Just like you, sweet pea," I was more enthralled with him than my scallops. "Talking of heritage and rooting, this smokiness conjures an image of a dream I'd once had."

In my late teens, just after my parents divorced, I'd dreamed about a group of gypsies. At first, I appeared to be watching a group of about twenty old people dressed in relatively drab, heavy clothing wandering in a lush forest spanning both banks of the most majestic river I'd ever seen. A mass of crystal clear water appeared to stand still – so deep and serene it glistened like an all-knowing oracle. It drew me in.

I stood, happy and content, at the end of one of two long, rustic, weathered wooden trestles. Like a voyeur peering through a telescope, the old biddies were laughing, joking, telling tales. Their faces were alive. Their opaque, blue eyes reflected the river's sparkle. Some graciously picked from large platters of colourful, pickled foods while others danced to old folk tunes strummed on a mandolin. I turned to take my leave.

"Hey!" A call stopped me dead in my tracks. I turned. An old Slavic man, aeons of wisdom projecting through mesmeric eyes and welcoming smile held out an old fiddle.

"Why don't you come play for us?"

As I told Dougal my dream, I realised it wasn't the emulsions' smokiness that had reminded me of it but the way my stomach fluttered and dropped at seeing his sheer delight. In the dream I'd felt as if I'd dropped into an abyss – but I was sublimely peaceful, as if I knew these old gypsies were my ancestors come to greet me. I felt like I'd belonged with them.

"That's what happens when you get rooted my wee gypsy girl," said Dougal, with a glint in his eyes. "Perhaps you'll play for me one day?"

"Meat, for you madam?" The waiter asked, placing my lamb loin and lamb belly, turnip, pickled Ramson's Seeds of wild garlic, and lamb cress. Dougal flashed me an expectant, cheeky grin.

"And for you Sir – seafood."

Poking the lamb loin, I glanced the waiter's rear walk away.

"Mmm, Irish or Scottish?" I said without lifting my head. Feeling Dougal's eyes upon me, I prodded the belly. "Mmm. Best stick with the Scottish, the belly's too fatty for me."

"At least I'm not slippery like this fish," he retorted.

"You know I'm kidding," I rejoined. "My man needs to be like this meat – flavoursome, firm, and wild."

"So, I'm in!" he laughed, lifting his fork and pulling a face that said "Hooray!"

"You shouldn't be so presumptuous," I teased. "You just suggested I'm a slippery fish! If that's so, you'd best prove you're firm, stable and trustworthy, right?"

"That's me," he replied with a shrug. "My people came down from the Isle of Skye and we've been in Scotland ever since."

"Too full for dessert," I said, rubbing my stomach. "Our usual?" We opted for a slate platter of hand selected local cheese and wine that enhanced its flavours.

"Ooh! An unusual selection," Dougal said. "Variety is definitely the spice of life."

I don't recall the wines that accompanied our foraging, but there wasn't a drop to return. Standards in service matched the enthusiasm exuded by staff as they talked through the technicalities of these treasured delights – the whole spontaneous event experience was truly a delight.

"A nightcap for you, my precious?"

= > < =

"Let's head off," Dougal called. "I've places to show you."

He eagerly introduced me to Galway's varied landscape of vast bogs, rivers, lakes and woodlands, rich meadows, rugged hills and dramatic mountains, each appealing to differing aspects of my imagination.

"Wow!" I said, as my eyes fell upon the stunning coastline of unpolluted clear blue waters and white sandy beaches. Holding back a tear of delight, "It's sensational."

We stood in Connemara's distinctly beautiful and desolate national park encased in the most hideous bright green 'penis head' plastic ponchos. Dougal slipped tight behind me, sheltering me from the gale force wind. One arm was wrapped across my chest, the other pointed out the waters of Killary Harbour, Galway Bay, and the Atlantic Ocean. Surrounded by the smell of the ocean and the thundering waters, we both found ourselves transported to different times and places. A fear of drowning in the dark, deep freezing water off South America rose swiftly to my mind, only to subside in the safe, comfortable warmth of Dougal's body pressed against mine. I felt Dougal's heart pound as he remembered a roar of excitement from northern Queensland's surfing beaches. We braced ourselves, laughing all the way, gripped hands for dear life – and, on the count of three, we leapt into the air, attempting to fly in the storm.

"Ah, for memories, eh?" he said, with a pang of nostalgia. "What they do for us!"

We stumbled and fumbled back to the car. Deserving a

winter warmer before heading back to Dublin, we stopped for a pint in the quintessential Irish town of Clifden, with its quirky shops, restaurants and traditional pubs.

"This was such a wonderful idea," I told Dougal, with beaming eyes and broad smile. "Happy girl!"

"Happy boy!" he replied, satiated.

With my Dougal, I always felt relaxed yet invigorated. We had all the time in the world to be or do whatever we chose – nothing was out of bounds. If our trip around Ireland taught me anything, it was that we were truly two of a kind. We were interested in the same things – history, culture, people and places. We shared the same desire – to drink the whole world in one gulp and then look around for more. Dougal certainly had the 'gift of the gab' but he rarely held court too long. There were never awkward pauses between us – we always had interesting, stupid or funny things to entertain us. We yakked our way around the countryside and back to Dublin's fair city.

We wandered through the famed Temple Bar area, stopping to sample local brews, traversing the city, crossing the River Liffey at the old iron Ha'penny Bridge. I took his hand through narrow lanes and streets, absorbing the lively atmosphere. By the statue of Molly Malone, Dougal pulled me to halt, smiling.

"You're my so pretty," he said, pecking my cheek and linking my arm in his. "I want to show you something in Trinity College. For some reason it reminds me of you."

He refused to give any more clues. We strolled through the lush grass and cobblestones of the College to the famed eighteenth century library, past the extraordinary Book of Kells where we stopped to ooh and ahh over its workmanship. It was like it was a treasure made just for us.

I sensed Dougal was on a mission. He dragged me over to a glass case filled with Lord Byron memorabilia where an original manuscript of the poet's work, *The Prisoner of Chillon* was kept. As I bent over to take a closer look at the type he leaned in.

"I think you and Byron are kindred spirits," he whispered in my ear.

"What do you mean?" I asked, surprised a little. "Am I mad, bad and dangerous to know. Or are you saying I'm like a gimpy nymphomaniac poet born almost two centuries ago who lived large but ended in a Greek tent with a mysterious fever?"

"No, you're a lifelong libertarian traveller finding solace in beauty who did everything her way," he sighed, rolling his eyes at me.

"Well, that's a bit more like it," I approved. Dougal reached for my hand again, pulling me away and reciting, "I love not Man the less, but Nature more." At least I agreed with Byron in that respect.

Satiated by history we made our way to St James Gate Guinness Brewery for some black gold to quench our thirst.

"We can't leave without supping from the source," Dougal insisted, getting us a pint while I snapped up a seat with a 360-degree view overlooking Dublin and beyond. It's true, once you've supped a Guinness from the source it's never as good again. As we sat sipping the perfectly drawn black gold, as it's so often called, I caught his eye.

"What's up? I asked, "You've become very pensive."

"I'd planned to keep my news until we're on the boat tonight," he said with the saddest blue eyes, taking my hand. I saw his struggle.

"Then do." I suggested, squeezing his hand with a heavy heart and a lump in my throat. "Whatever's easiest for you." It was obviously bad news – for one if not both of us.

Dougal turned and met my eyes. "There's been a major fall out with the partners," he said. "Things are a mess and I need a fresh start – a clean slate."

"What do you mean by a 'clean slate'?" I asked, already knowing. But I needed to hear him tell it, I didn't want to leave any room for misinterpretation.

"Clean. Cheese board clean," he clarified with glazed eyes. "Things are dire. It's going to take me a while to resolve matters and get back on top. I can't take you with me. It'll be a struggle to take care of myself, Kim."

I'd wanted to suggest we could work things out together, but my throat jammed. I'd understood exactly what he meant by 'clean slate,' I knew him well enough. He was going to cut all communications. He had his own way of doing things. He needed to focus. He'd manage his affairs alone, in his own sweet time and I'd be a worry and a distraction.

I had a million questions but no breath with which to ask them. I reached for my glass and thought better of it – my stomach had turned. I was hollow.

"I've taken a job down South. I'm so sorry Kim," he said, dejected. "I promise I'll be in touch as soon as I can."

"I don't like it. I don't want you to go," I managed to squeak out. "But I understand. I really do!"

"Don't worry," he said, "We'll be all right. 'Love will find a way through paths where wolves fear to prey'," quoting Byron.

=><=

Our double berth cabin with two single beds was a squeeze. Neither of us complained. We happily huddled because we knew it would be our last night together – even if everything was all at sea.

Despite my emotional turmoil, I began to feel incredibly calm. My heart had stopped racing, my breath was back to normal – somehow I just felt our story wasn't over, that everything would work out. Not today and maybe not tomorrow but someday.

"So, what will you do now?" Dougal asked. "Get another contract?"

"Probably," I mused. "Or maybe I'll try something else

entirely – pursue my dream job? Corporate life isn't what it's cracked up to be – at least not for me."

"I think you should write, like Byron," he said, then as I started to scoff turned to me and added, "No, wait a minute – listen. You're well travelled, knowledgeable about history, geography and so much else. And you've got a great sense of humour. Why not?"

"I doubt there's much of a living to be had from it these days – unless you'd be willing to send food stamps to a starving artist?" I asked.

"I'll miss you," he said quietly.

"And I you, my lovely," I replied, a solemn tear falling.

"No matter," he whispered in my ear, wiping it away. "You'll always have the last quarter inch of my heart."

And, despite our sadness, we reminisced about better times and laughed our way home across the Irish Sea.

$$=><=$$

The day after Dougal and I returned from our time in Dublin he moved south. I was devastated but accepting. I knew it was for the best. After all it wouldn't be long before I left Scotland myself for Holland, in pursuit of my own dream.

"No matter," he'd whispered in my ear, wiping away my tears. "You'll always have the last quarter inch of my heart."

$$===><===$$

6
SPAIN

I was on my last leg, literally. MS had attacked again and my leg was a heavy, motionless lump of dead meat. I was immobilised. After a few days of lifting and laying the dead meat, feeling began to return and I was able to move around again — of sorts.

I'd seen a number of specialists since the delightful Dr George diagnosed my condition but none had his compassion. Sitting down in front of my new doctor I watched her review my medical history.

"I like to see for myself," said Dr Harriet. "We'll re-run the tests – if you don't mind?"

At last, I thought with relief – a neurologist who treats me like a person rather than an inconvenience or statistic. Her demeanour was so different to the others I'd seen – mostly men who appeared more interested in their research. In her skirt, blouse, jumper and statement spectacles, she seemed more accessible. Her dark overtones and angular face suggested an Eastern European heritage.

When we'd first met she'd made me feel I was the only thing in the world that mattered, that I had her complete attention and she had my trust. To me, Dr Harriet wasn't just a specialist – she was special. Highly recommended by my local GP, I wanted to know more about her (especially as she was privy to all my MS secrets). I was curious why she became a neurologist. I'd wanted to ask but refrained from taking too much of her valuable time, for which I'd be billed.

"Now, let's see. I have a few things to show you," she said, turning her monitor in my direction.

As I leaned forward, not wanting to miss a thing, Dr Harriet methodically scrolled through a series of images, pointing to areas of interest. So far, so good. No issues. Nothing new. I relaxed my guard as Dr Harriet's eyes flicked between the screen and me, comparing the abnormal spots on my brain and along my spine. They were mostly grey, varying in size and colour.

"All's good then?" I asked, repositioning myself, thinking we'd finished.

A new image flashed upon the screen. My gaze locked onto one large, bright, white spot. Stunned, I watched the little white arrow move slowly across to it.

"Another attack, here, will probably take your legs. And there'll be nothing we can do," Dr Harriet explained.

Whatever else she said next, that was all I heard.

=><=

After Canada, I'd tried to find suitable work, but I'd had trouble finding the right position. I wanted to work for a global body, more specifically one of the United Nations organisations. I'd believed the Masters Program and the connections I'd made would help. Determined to secure work where my skills would be put to great use, I submitted resumes with carefully crafted letters, selectively targeting decision makers. Again, my applications disappeared into a black hole — this time, the universal black hole of the public sector.

So I ended up back in financial services.

I threw myself full swing into work, willing that white spot to disappear. There were project milestones to schedule, issue logs to get under control, risks to avert and communications underway. If I focussed only on moving forward then surely my brain could convince that white spot into remission – almost daily the media reported the miracle powers of positive thinking. I prided myself on my 'do or die' attitude, so why not a miracle for me?

But no matter how frantically I worked, however much I got done, I felt flat and uninspired. It didn't help that the British tabloids were full of social discontent and international woes, either. The weather in Glasgow matched my mood perfectly – dark, dank and breathtakingly cold.

"I've had enough," I said turning to Rhona. We'd been working solidly on a mind numbingly complex project all day without a break. Fresh air and time-out were most definitely required. Flashing me a conspiratorial grin, she slapped down her laptop screen and stood up.

We took a brisk walk around the company's winter wonderland grounds to warm ourselves up and clear out the cobwebs, then brushed thick snow from a park bench and perched gazing out on the distant silhouette of Stirling Castle. It was so cold I'm surprised our breath didn't freeze. I found solace in the Trossachs and the simple lines of the dark, foreboding castle set against the hillside above me. Its renaissance and medieval structure stood grandly curvaceous high above the city, overlooking the River Forth. Staring up, I felt connected to the almost mystical force that seemed to emanate from its ramparts.

"Rhona, there must be more to life than this," I said gloomily. It wasn't that I didn't like my work. It was the atmosphere, or lack of, that made me feel overwhelmingly that I needed to escape. I was feeling cooped up, sedentary, uncreative — stuck starring at screens all day was certainly not my idea of fun. Right then and there, I started planning my next adventure.

Time was running out – I needed to get moving on my plans for an alternative life, to see more of the world – before my legs no longer worked.

=><=

I'd been putting my affairs in order prior to heading off to Australia when I found a magazine article I'd written after a Tai Chi conference in France. It ignited memories of wonderful times full of sunshine, laughter, activity, health and happiness in Jasnières in the Vallée de al Loire, where forty of us had spent a week by the lake, training barefoot on soft, lush, green grass, shaded from the intense afternoon sun by dense coppices and drinking wonderful French wine. What better way to begin my quest to see everything the world had to offer with a healthy, stress-free retreat somewhere warm?

I called Jimmy.

"Hello. It's been a while. How are you? What have you been up to?" he asked, without pause.

Jimmy intrigued me. A little guy, fair haired with a hint of copper – probably remnants of a red headed Scottish lineage, or possibly Irish, given his opaque green eyes, his wee 'gemmie' appearance was such a contradiction to his gentle personality. I'd never have believed him to be a Tai Chi Instructor.

He was also the consummate wheeler and dealer – always up to something. Whatever you needed, Jimmy could source – information, goods, contacts, anything. He was one of the good guys. Once I'd mentioned to him I'd been searching everywhere for books based on the Japanese television show, Monkey. Before I knew it, I was the excited owner of a superb set – three special edition books, perfectly presented in their green and gold sleeves.

"Oh, you know how it is – all sorts and nothing much really," I replied vaguely. I didn't want to go into my health problems – I didn't want him to have second thoughts about inviting me to join the group. "Just calling to see if you guys still train together, and if you're going to Jasnières this year?"

"Actually, we're heading to Coria, Spain in a week's time. Coming?" he asked, jokingly.

"Sure am!

Perfect. I was on my way.

$$= > < =$$

"Tickets please, have your tickets ready," the inspector repeatedly called as he walked the aisle clipping tickets with his nifty wee hole punch. "You do know it's much cheaper to buy a return?" he offered when he took my ticket.

"Not if you're only going one way," I smiled.

"Do you live in Spain, then?"

"No. Afterwards I'm travelling on to Australia," I said, wishing he'd move on to clip the next ticket. I didn't want to be rude, but my plans weren't up for discussion with the entire carriage. "Then, who knows where!" I said, mysteriously.

"Nice for some," he said with a sniff, reaching for the next ticket.

I'd reserved a cabin to escape the crowds and weather the next stage of my journey — a 24-hour sail to Santander, Spain. I wanted a peaceful passage, not to be constantly disturbed by those who don't travel so well on high seas. So, by the time we docked, I was well rested.

Energised and excited, I disembarked with a clutch of tourism pamphlets and timetables. During the long crossing I'd researched plenty of sights and activities to scout before joining the Tai Chi team near the Portuguese border. I was determined to check every box on my carefully curated wishlist of places to visit — who knew if I'd make it back this way. But I decided to take it easy, too – 'relaxed and effortless' activities won over 'see and do' that time.

I headed west to my first stop – Las Médulas, an impressive landscape with stunningly deep, ochre coloured shards of raw earth towering above dark green vegetation that looked rich, intense and dramatic. It had a power that was indefinable, like I was peering into another world, one completely man-made. Around 2,000 years ago, the Romans' search for gold had led them to redesign the natural terrain so they could carry gold nuggets down the mountainside into the lower rivers. Through great feats of engineering they had used nature to filter the gold via a complicated system of pulleys, levers and aqueducts that washed tonnes of soft sandstone until the precious metal shone through.

As I stood on the observation deck overlooking the trails below at the glorious chestnut and hazelnut trees that had grown up amongst the tailings, I adopted the Roman's ingenuity as a metaphor for my own travels. Like them, I would with each step, consciously follow their process, slowly washing the soft sandstone of my outer layers I'd reveal my own mettle. Suddenly I felt that, like the old song, I'd packed up my troubles in my old kit bag. I was clear-headed – MS, work or the world's woes were furthest from my mind. I stood, soaking up the most wonderful sublime feeling. The familiar 'me' had returned – I was free again. A load had been lifted off my shoulders – and while I was still apprehensive about the course of my illness, I was also curious about the future and what it had in store.

Predictably, my euphoria was short lived. I descended to the rocky trail below but must have hurried too much, because my feet came out from under me, sending me off track, both physically and mentally. I felt like an insignificant bundle of twigs lost in a recreated landscape. Frozen, unable to move, I was suddenly very, very tired of having to pick myself up.

"Why me?' I groaned, daring the universe to answer

meaningfully. I wanted the ground to swallow me whole, the heavens to render me senseless. As I struggled to get my limbs to work, I tried to negotiate with the powers that be.

"Just give me a little more time and I promise I'll do my job," I growled. "And if you could see your way through to sending me a gold nugget – not necessarily the Roman kind, just some kind of good fortune…"

I waited. Nope. They weren't listening. It was up to me to find my own power.

A psychosomatic therapy course once taught me, 'your issues are in your tissues'. Your physical body carries your emotions. I'd inherited the stiff upper lip English trait, well and truly. I didn't feel comfortable expressing strong emotions – I rarely yelled; actually, I rarely voiced a thing. I never saw the point – no one seemed to hear me anyhow. It was like I had no power to my voice – perhaps that was why people often ignored me when I was speaking.

"You wouldn't say 'boo, to a goose," my mother always said.

I'd learned how to stay quiet as a child the day my grandfather shut me up. I had parked myself opposite him at the honey oak table in the dining room. I was following the glistening streaks of the table's grain, like fools gold, swinging my feet, chin resting on folded arms as sunlight streamed through the large, small paned windows and cast shadows over my Grandmother's potted germaniums. I don't think she had much of a green thumb, as they never looked very healthy to me. The room smelled of silver polish and I'd chatter away as my Grandfather worked on his accounts. 'Chatterbox' was his nickname for me.

That is until the day he snapped at me to stop talking or get out. Just like that, with no warning. Perhaps, swinging my legs under the table wasn't such a good idea. Or, maybe I'd disturbed his concentration as he ran two fingers up the page? I was shocked and surprised – his normally benign good nature had switched in an instant. What had I done to deserve it? I'd been called 'shy' ever since.

But there, at the bottom of the rocky trail in Las Médulas, I decided to let my voice rip.

"Alright. That's it!" I wailed to the gods. "Don't save me. I'll create my own bloody miracles."

I wasn't going to feel sorry for myself. I wouldn't let MS lick me. I'd stay strong and continue, doing exactly what I wanted – my way, in my own sweet time. And I was going to start right then, right there.

Suddenly I could feel the power in my limbs returning. I dragged myself up slowly, dusted off the stones and twigs I'd collected and began the long walk back with a new sense of purpose.

I'd found my power.

=><=

Zamora was like walking into a movie set depicting the Middle Ages. Crossing the River Duero at the Puente de Piedra (stone bridge) I was surrounded by archetypal medieval structures, many perfectly intact. The city had withstood long periods of siege for its 'triple defensive ring' of gates — the outstanding Portillo de la Traición, the Puerta de Doña Urraca and the Puerta del Obispo.

Traversing the cobbled streets, I encountered vaults with Gothic arches, apses and doorways decorated with plant motifs, including some of the cities oldest reliefs — around every charming corner there was more. Zamora's history was recorded in its architecture, design and detailed decor. Throughout the ages, each ruler had made his mark on the city's character until it seemed like an unplanned cacophony of bespoke structures. Each age had drawn upon earlier architectural elements and increased in geometric complexity, especially the magnificent domes resting on humungous piers and the elegant mosaics, which had replaced earlier, more cumbersome carvings.

As I wandered, I began to see the parallels with my own life. I, too, was a palimpsest – the result of hundreds if not thousands of messages, some hastily written and removed just as quickly, some carefully built up over years of development. I was the sum of a plethora of diverse experiences – physical, emotional and spiritual. Each contributed to form my character and inform my understanding of self.

Even MS had a role to play. Without it, I wouldn't have been standing in that cobblestone street, trying to make sense of the sights, sounds and smells that accosted me. I'd have still been in a dank little office in Stirling, wondering if there was more to life. Without it, would I have realised what I wanted out of life? Would I have had the courage to step out of my comfort zone, again and again, without its Damocles sword hanging over me?

"Your life might be fun. But a rolling stone gathers no moss," one friend had politely chided me for living the way I do. "You need to stay still; start your inner journey."

"Do I?" I replied, as if to say, 'You have no idea what's going on in here.'

Unlike many of those old buildings, I may not have gathered much external moss but I was the proud owner of an exclusive, internal arboretum – a spaghetti junction of thoughts and feelings, hopes and fears. There was more than I could ever hope to unravel, more beneath the surface that no one saw. But I felt like I was beginning to understand.

$$= > < =$$

I enjoyed travelling across Spain by bus — the air-con helped. Like the Australian outback, the Spanish landscape is, on the face of it, fairly monotonous. But, beyond the churches, plazas and cobbled streets lies Pandora's box — each region, town and city offers something unique.

Across the main square, I targeted Salamanca's oldest café, Café Novelty, which had first opened in 1905. It was far more than a café – through the brass revolving door, a chic interior where, to the right - merchants, stock-breeders, manufacturers and rightists had participated in the daily tertulia (a social gathering with literary, artistic or political overtones), and to the left – liberals, medics, lawyers and academics from the historic local university of Salamanca. The round salon with it's coloured, atrium hosted dances, orchestral events and opulent weddings. Café Novelty was splendid – until the 1936 Spanish Civil War. Its clientele was as much divided as the country – some were exiled, some executed and others took shelter, but the majority joined General Franco and it was renamed Café National.

"Hola, Senorita," called a dashing waiter as I approached the café.

"Hola!" I replied with a nod and friendly smile.

"Quieres una bebida?" he said, shaking his hand to suggest a drink.

"Si," I replied, without a thought. He was gorgeous – if there were ever a stereotypical Spanish waiter, he was it. His red cummerbund was positioned to accentuate his small waist atop long silhouetted legs and his solid torso peeked from an open-necked, crisp white shirt. He was tall, dark and handsome – a sight for sore eyes. And a dry throat.

"Vino blanco, por favor."

"Una copa de vino?" He questioned with a smirk. "No, no es posible!"

"Por que no?" I said as I shrugged my shoulders and raised my hands, palms up.

The waiter mirrored my movements with a mysterious look: "El famous bodega – ido!"

"Gone!" I said. Had I misunderstood?

"Si. Ido! En 1963. The restaurant was closed and the wine depository, shut down," he laughed in perfect, accented English. "You know the history of Café Novelty?"

In the 1970s, the café was repaired and again became a centre of political secrecy. Remote salons accommodated subversive anti-Franco ideologists writing their manifestos. By 1978 the café had closed again, but was back again by 1979, redecorated to evoke its bygone splendour.

"Would you like to eat?" he asked, presenting a colourful menu.

"Yes. I would," I replied immediately. Half a dozen roasted chestnuts were not going to sustain me much longer.

Entering through the revolving door was like stepping back in time – very art deco, the large black and white tiled floors gleamed, tall marble columns stood equidistance along the bar. Wood framed mirrors, old street scenes, and sepia portraits lined the walls. From the ceiling hung large white glass globes, suspended on metal arched frames. The décor was just as I'd imagined – but as an old acquaintance once said, 'You never know who you're going to meet.' I chuckled to myself. Positioned by his favourite seat stood a memorial statue of Gonzalo Torrente Ballester, a local Spanish professor and author who frequented the café for twenty-five years and helped its return to a place of influence in the cultural life of Salamanca.

"So, what else is worth seeing, here?" I asked the waiter as he served me tapas, local wine and a local culinary speciality – regional-styled rice, stuffed hake and custard with almonds in the beautiful, perfectly fashioned setting, over looking the Plaza Mayor de Salamanca.

"The Old Cathedral," he said pointing at a Romanesque/Gothic style building. "Started building in twelfth century, completed in the fourteenth."

"And that one," he added, pointing to another. "The new

cathedral – similar story, begun in seventeenth century Gothic style, and continued with a less showy Baroque style into the eighteenth century."

"Two hundred years? To build a cathedral!" I exclaimed. I was gob-smacked at the thought of tradesmen working on those magnificent buildings for so long. I wondered how they must have felt knowing they would never see the fruition of their labour. I attempted, theoretically, to stand in their shoes – Yes, times were different then. Things did take longer – seemingly a lot longer. But, they, I was certain were true craftsmen – of what we'd call traditional techniques. No instant gratification there. I'd have been stuffed! I was a natural project worker – get a job, do the job, leave the job. That's not to say I couldn't stick with the same job for a long time. But I needed to feel there was progress and variety in my work. As, I do in all aspects of life. What was it Dougal had said? 'Variety is the spice of life?' I wasn't mentally equipped to maintain the status quo. Which probably meant I would have been quite content working alongside those traditional builders. Like them, I suspect, I would have had the same passion, pride and purpose. But unfortunately, I had a date – had to keep rolling along.

"How come you know so much about these old buildings?" I asked, amazed by his local knowledge and enthusiasm in full flight.

"I'm studying medieval architecture at the university," he explained. "Waiting pays the bills while I study."

Nodding, I looked over the perfectly fashioned Plaza Mayor de Salamanca, enjoying a break after a long day on my feet.

"You should stay a while," the waiter ventured. "There's a lot going on around here."

"I'd love to but I can't," I replied. "I'm just passing through."

=><=

Tai Chi

Jimmy lifted me off the ground and twirled me around. By the time I'd reached Coria, I felt I'd been on the road forever. The taxi dropped me off in a small out-of-the-way village called Santos and I walked the long, narrow, uphill strip of dry dusty road to the centre. It was hot and I was exhausted — but in a good way. I was ready to catch up with long lost mates and reap the rewards of Tai Chi Chuan.

"Hey, I thought you were kidding. I never thought you'd come," he exclaimed.

"So, you don't remember me, then," I jibbed.

"I can't believe you're here. Come on, let's get you settled in," he said, taking my bag in one hand and placing his arm around my shoulder he walked me to reception.

Jimmy expected around fifty delegates in total. The usual core, twenty-five or so, were from Europe – Britain, Italy, Germany and Holland. The remaining delegates would stay for a week or two.

"How long are you with us?" asked the check-in Queen at the registration desk with a beautiful welcoming smile.

"Four weeks," I replied, feeling hyped.

"Lucky you," she said. "Here's tomorrow's schedule – reduced, I'm afraid – most people arrive the day after." I took a quick glance then Jimmy and I set off to find my room.

At the end of a hand-built stone structure, it had no need for frames or glass windows – a hole provided natural air con that combated the year round heat. It had a stunning view across the dry terrain, none the worse for lack of greenery. The local slate floor was heaven on earth – it cooled the soles of my hot, weary feet – bliss in forty plus degrees. A single bed, set in the middle of the room, waited to be made up with freshly laundered linen folded neatly and placed upon the pillows. In the corner stood a simple clothes rail. It was all I needed – clean, functional and basic.

Santos was an oasis. Its beautifully tended gardens were filled with local plants and plenty of full-canopied trees to provide shade from the intense Extremadura sun. And, while the accommodation was rustic, the fodder was fit for royalty. I was treated to endless Middle Eastern salads, chickpeas and crumbled feta sprinkled with lemon, sumac and fresh parsley from the garden, home grown roasted beetroot and onions drizzled with olive oil and shredded spicy lamb, jumbled together with freshly sun ripened tomatoes. Delicious!

After lunch I found a quiet shady spot by the lake to doze and strategise how to make the most of my week. Should I stick with one form or train in a selection?

"Instead of all your chopping and changing, if you'd stuck with one subject, you'd be running the country, by now," my grandmother had once said. I took my cue from her and decided I'd focus on Tai Chi. Once mastered, there's no excuse not to practise. It only takes one square foot – a gym on the square.

Tai Chi Chuan, commonly referred to as Tai Chi, is much more than the aesthetically pleasing movements seen by non-practitioners — a simple 'meditative' exercise to a realistic martial art. At the conference, our instructors, trainers and practitioners covered the full gambit of forms — the slow, hand form with movements most commonly seen practiced in China's parks, Qigong exercises and meditation, Pushing Hands or Tui Shou, training for combat and various martial artists. Each had something to share. There was always a lively conversation to join should it take your fancy; the heavily debated concept of Qi (Chi) energy — the basis of the 2,000 years old, Traditional Chinese Medicine (TCM) with its principles of Yin and Yang, meridians that carry Qi energy through the body, and our ability to unblock imbalances through practice usually livened free time. Someone always played devils advocate. It was easy to pick the dedicated from those who, like me, were less balanced, less co-ordinated and less supple; my meridians must have been dammed, not blocked.

Tai Chi, doesn't require great strength or flexibility, it's largely based on technique. It can be carried out individually or in groups – a complete work out. Feet shoulder width apart, the practitioner moves with slightly flexed knees working the thigh muscles and hamstrings. Spine erect. Deep, soft rhythmic breathing calms the energy flow – to begin. Slow, controlled, repetitive movements shift the body weight, bringing strength to the core, upper body, back and abdomen, and an improved posture. Perfectly synchronised. Balance. Muscle Tone. Relaxed. And alert – all in one square foot. Who needs gyms?

Tai Chi's underlying principles lie with Yinyang (yin-yang). Like many other Chinese philosophical notions, the influences of yinyang are easy to observe but its conceptual meanings are hard to define. Despite the differences in interpretation, application, and appropriation there are three basic themes: the coherent fabric of nature and mind, exhibited in all existence; the jiao (interaction) between the waxing and waning of the cosmic and human realms, and the process of harmonisation ensuring constant, dynamic balance of all things. As the Zhuangzi (Chuang-tzu) claims, 'Yin is freezing in its highest form, while yang is boiling in its' lowest – the chill comes from heaven while the warm comes from the earth; their interaction establishes 'he' (harmony), giving birth to all things. The popular yinyang symbol, a circle where equally proportioned black and white intertwines, represents the balance of equal opposites. No one claimed specific ownership of the symbol despite its rich textual and visual history inspired by a primeval vision of cosmic harmony. Chinese thinkers have sought to codify the underlying pattern since the Han dynasty (206BC — 220 AD).

Everyone knows exercise is good for you. But Dr George had warned me that many people with chronic conditions often find participation and motivation difficult – especially if their bodies are dysfunctional. Although doctors once advised those with MS to avoid physical activity, we now know exercise is beneficial – it can increase muscle strength, mobility and positive mood and decrease fatigue so you have better quality of life.

"I'd recommend Tai Chi," he said. "It's proven to help reduce pain, stress and anxiety. And benefits tend to increase over time."

Someone once told me that the most predictable thing about MS is its unpredictability. How do you live with that? As Nike would say, "Just do it!"

= > < =

"Hey, Kim," called Jimmy. "What did you do today?"
"Not enough," I replied. I'd been pretty lazy, spending most of the day settling in and catching up with the guys. But I'd done the early morning 'kick-start' session, then a Tai Chi session, followed by a bit of push hands, with chat.

"More chat than play?" he asked. I nodded in the affirmative.
"That's ma girl," he said, clipping the back of my head.

'If you only knew,' I thought. The early morning start proved to be worthwhile – an eye opener, you could say. I thought I'd tracked pretty well with my balance and co-ordination. It turned out not to be the case. Stance? Check. Posture? Check. Foot Plant? Check. But I kept falling down.

"Pissed again!" I called. Nervous, I laughed out loud, but internally I wasn't feeling the joke. I felt like Pinocchio 'with no strings to hold me up, to pick me up …! '

"Jimmy, thank you so much for the invitation," I said one evening after a delicious meal of grilled sardines, crispy green leaf salad, cous cous mixed with roast veg, delicately diced – filling, light and easy.

Spain | 109

"Of course. It's been a long time, but we never forget our friends." I felt tears prick my eyes. "Hey, what's up?" He asked.

"Oh, nothing really. I've just had a bit of a hard time recently. You have no idea how happy I was that you remembered me when I called. Your invitation meant the world

I'd forgotten how much you and the guys meant to me," I said. "You made my day Jimmy. I felt like I belonged somewhere."

"But you do," he clarified, "You'll always be one of the team," Jimmy claimed. He gestured for me to sit with him. We sat in comradely silence, each in our own worlds. I contemplated how much I had needed to belong somewhere, anywhere. Let me rephrase that. I felt like I fitted in everywhere but I belonged nowhere. I was never lonely but always alone. It seemed to me that I was always on a different page, dancing a different tune, out of sync with everyone else. I sometimes wondered who'd pick me up when I fell down.

"It's not as though I haven't got on — I'm proud of what I've done. I know I make my own decisions, but I can't resist the compulsion to follow my nose — it's like Fairground Attraction – 'the wind knows my name, and it's calling me, calling me, again' to search for something, somewhere I'll feel at home," I'd explained.

"Kim, sounds to me you need to find your culture," suggested Jimmy.

"You know – maybe you're right." I laughed,

I remembered how I'd often said to my grandmother, "One day, Nan. One day I'll find it."

"Find what?" she'd ask.

"I don't know, but I will when I've found it — it's probably my grave," I'd say, and she would, obligingly, be amused.

In more recent years, I've known how anxious and overwhelming it can be. I use to have a recurring dream: I was a young boy walking through the desert looking for my community when in the distance I spotted lights. I hastened to find myself at the edge of a cliff — I couldn't get across. Later I saw myself as a robbed old man, nestled alone in the corner of ancient crumbled ruins, dying alone. I knew they were only dreams, but they struck a chord. I needed to find my 'home'.

"There's something you're not telling me – right?" Jimmy's question startled me out of my thoughts. I looked up, surprised at his prescience.

"Yeah, I wanted to ask you about Tai Chi and MS – you up for it?" I said, looking at him sideways. His mouth dropped open in surprise.

"You?" he said, with a haunted look, "Are you on meds?"

"No. They want me to, but I just can't do it, Jimmy," I explained. Back on the bus, I'd gazed across the vast plains of tobacco near the Jarandilla de la Vera, where workers in the distance satisfying their thirst by drinking from the 'botijo' (a traditional earthenware jug) as they harvested in the searing heat. They were selecting dark leaves from the base of the tobacco plants and loading them into the gua-gua (the farm tractor trailer used for transporting the tobacco). The ripe tobacco leaves would then be taken for drying on a stove or hung in the traditional way, upside down, in the drying barns.

I imagined, one day, perhaps in my lifetime, all the tobacco plantations producing marijuana – for medicinal purposes of course.

"There are a number of drugs …" I recalled my conversation with Dr Harriet.

"Drugs!" went off in my head like an explosion. Horrified, my stomach churned. I didn't even take aspirins. How could I spend my life on drugs?

" … I recommend you talk to the administrators and then we can see what suits you best," she continued.

I had felt like a meltdown was imminent. But I stayed in control. I stayed focused.

"Are you crazy?" Jimmy exclaimed, when I told him that I was refusing meds. "Won't they keep you from getting worse?"

"Probably," I laughed. "But, in all seriousness, I did the research, asked all the questions and received unconvincing answers – so I made a call. It was a tough decision – one of the hardest I've ever made."

"Well, Tai Chi isn't a cure. But, there are heaps of benefits, as you well know," confirmed Jimmy.

"Best get training, then," I said, jumping up and heading towards the exercise field.

=><=

Despite my early setbacks, it wasn't long before it all returned to me — I was soon relaxed, sure-footed and back in the swing. The martial artists were a delight to watch and partner training had couples calm and relaxed, pushing and yielding as arms flailed in the energy, remaining sensitive to the movements or intention of their opponent until a raucous laugh signalled that one had won out. The San Shou practitioners heated things up a little — fast forceful strikes negated by soft yielding actions. Then there were the weapon forms: traditional straight swords, broadswords and staffs and the adaptations, cane, fan and short or long stick.

There was no doubt in my mind that yin had chilled me – it had dealt me the short stick. Everything about me at that moment said 'normal' – the picture of health and happiness. But (there's always a 'but'), I'd lost confidence in my feet. I mean I didn't know where they were. Yes, I knew they were at the end of my legs, but you try walking when you can't feel your feet. Drop. Stumble. Bump. Jeered for being clumsy, un-coordinated or seemingly drunk.

Since coming to Spain I'd learned to manage; I'd look at the ground, watch, then place one foot before I transferred my weight. Each step was measured, but there was a bright side. I'd started trying to use this enforced wariness to stop and take in everything that was around me. No more racing for me without legs that wouldn't do as asked – no more just passing though. I'd smell the roses, drink in each moment, see the trees not the forest – all those familiar clichés. I knew that one day MS could come to collect without warning. But in the meantime I'd make the most of each second I had.

At the end of the day I sought Jimmy out again.

"You know me pretty well," I said. "Would you help me shed some light on something? I've been trying to figure why I'm not getting anywhere. I've tried so hard, with so many failed opportunities, I feel I'm bashing my head against a brick wall."

"Did you ever read the books I got for you, about Monkey?" Jimmy asked. I thought about the set of leather bound books he'd got me, featuring a Sun Wu Kong (Monkey) caricature etched in gold leaf on each cover. Written during the sixteenth century, The Journey to the West is a Chinese literary classic set in the seventh century. It tells the story a Buddhist disciple who was banished from heavenly paradise for slighting the Buddha's Law and sentenced to spend ten lifetimes on earth practicing religious self-cultivation. In his last lifetime, he reincarnates as Xuan Zang (also known as Tang Monk and Tripitaka), who is asked by the Chinese emperor to retrieve the holy Mahayana Buddhist scriptures from the west. Because Xuan Zang is ill-equipped for such perilous travel, the goddess Guanyin arranges for three spirits banished from the heavens to protect him: the valiant but impetuous Monkey King (Sun Wu Kong), the lustful Pigsy, the taciturn Sand Monk, and the White Dragon Horse. This is their one chance to return to their celestial home.

The monkey, pig, fish and horse have their work cut out for them. Everyone wants to get their hands on Xuan Zang because it's rumoured his flesh can impart immortality. So the eclectic group encounter eighty-one trials on their journey – but in the end the pilgrims triumph, head back to China with sacred scriptures, and return to their rightful places in the heavens.

"Yep, Sun Wu Kong's my hero. He's such a cool dude," I replied. The Monkey King was born out of a rock, and learned supernormal powers from a Taoist master. With his mischievous nature and great powers, he created chaos both in heaven and the underworld. The heavenly Jade Emperor tried to calm him down by granting him the title of "Great Sage of Heaven," but Monkey couldn't control himself. Defiant, he wreaked havoc, challenging everything and everyone that crossed his path. He was determined to do things his way.

"Well, I think you should read them again. Take time to think about him – you're just like him," Jimmy offered.

"Are you saying I'm a defiant troublemaker who challenges everything?" I asked, nervously.

"They say the truth hurts," he rejoined, walking away.

Jimmy was right – in a way. I'd long fancied myself as the Monkey King – an energetic, spontaneous, fun-loving character who stood up against injustice. I related to that. Like Monkey I too had set off on a journey. Since childhood, I'd had a defiant streak, my demon devil – called upon only for the greater good, of course. Unfortunately, my chequered, unstable past had failed to teach me the art of diplomacy so my defiant ways were often misinterpreted. If only I'd been better understood – better connected. All in all, I was happy being likened to Monkey. He'd proven a critical asset to the monk. He could see right through the demons and their witchcraft, and wasn't tempted by beauty or riches. His wit helped the monk escape many a perilous situation. And although he proved unruly at times, he was later crowned "Buddha Victorious in Strife" for his great accomplishments.

I just wished I'd had his sense of purpose.

=><=

Over the four weeks in Santos, I'd made significant progress. I had greater awareness of my feet, better balance, improved co-ordination and greater flexibility – it was as though I'd been given a complete loom – a new neural network. But, beyond the obvious I felt so much stronger – physically and mentally. I stood taller – my posture had definitely improved. And I was back on form. Hoorah!

Blindsided, an arm came from behind to link through mine.

"Hey, I thought that was you," cried Amber, an old sparing partner from Jasnières. Amber and I had known each other a long time – I felt bad that we'd lost touch. She was a sacro-cranial practitioner. Using gentle touch the practitioner manipulates the skull joints, spine and pelvis to relieve pain and tension, harmonising the flow of spinal fluid, returning its natural rhythm to the central nervous system. It was a practice I knew traditional medics called pseudoscience, quackery.

I was so happy to see her. I wasn't at all surprised when I'd heard her clinic in Austria had been doing very well. She was beautiful – a lovely, gentle, caring person. I often wondered whether her professional skills provided credibility for the more unconventional therapies she offered, such as Reiki – a form of massage that I've never understood. It seemed a bit too remote for my liking; I was all about a hands on – feel the results approach. Nonetheless, Amber was an intelligent, honest and trustworthy woman whom I liked very much.

"I hope you don't mind, but Jimmy said you've had a hard time of late?" she said, creating an opportunity for me to tell her about it, should I choose.

"No, I don't mind," I replied. "I guess he told you I have MS?"

"Do you want to talk about it?" she asked.

"Actually, you could help me with something else that's been on my mind – if you're up for it?"

"Sure. Let's find a quiet spot in the garden," she suggested.

Despite her squat stature – about five feet nothing, broad and toned with a little extra weight around her middle since we'd last met, Amber hadn't fundamentally changed.

"It's often said things come in threes – well, I've figured there are three things I need in life," I told her. "I've called them my three P's – people, place, and purpose."

"You've been thinking! That explains a lot," she laughed.

"Yes. I've had my fair share of time on buses, boats and train, recently," I explained.

"We all need relationships," I went on. "No woman's an island – right? I mean, we need to be loved – whatever that means, I'm not sure. But I feel even a sense of being loved, having people around you that really care, could suffice. It's the connection – I think."

Amber listened intently as I continued.

"Which brings me to place. I need somewhere to call 'home' – a place to belong, a place to settle and find some internal peace. You know, somewhere you fit in, sharing the same values with those around you," I said.

"Where everybody knows your name?" Amber sang. I smiled, nodding.

"That brings me to purpose," I continued. "What's the point of anything if you don't have purpose?"

"My, you really have been thinking!" exclaimed Amber.

"But my real issue is – why can't I secure all three? I often, get one or two but the third consistently escapes me. I'm tired – I want to settle, before it's too late." I told her.

Amber paused, gathering her thoughts.

"It seems to me you want it all – and there's nothing wrong with that," she said. "But is it realistic?"

"I understand you need yin to appreciate yang, good to appreciate bad. Without black there is no white. But I don't understand why we can't have it all," I said, frustrated.

"Life is like the moon," she proselytised. "It waxes and wanes. You know that!"

"Yes. I understand nature's cycles. But surely, I should be able to have a modicum of fulfilment at any one time?" I asked.

"It seems to me, Kim – you want everything waxing, all the time." Amber started. "The laws of nature don't work that way – instead they strike a delicate balance. And, I believe you need to find yours. Control your dreams and understand what you're willing to sacrifice – you can't have it all, all of the time, unless …"

"You know the Baby Grand Master and his '3 nails technique'?" she added, gesturing to push hands. Known as The Baby Grand, William C. C. Chen wrote, "As a teenager, I was very fascinated by all those imaginative martial arts novels, movies and kung-fu handbooks popular with my generation. My most ambitious dream was to learn martial arts from a great master." Chen fulfilled his dream, as the youngest disciple of the great Cheng Man-Ching Chen. He excelled in tai chi and learned special, internal training – carried out three times a day; early morning, noon and late in the evening. Eventually his 'iron body' could absorb full force blows without injury. He could take any punch on his upper torso, rocks could be broken on him and motorcycles driven across his abdomen. His relaxed punches and kicks were extremely fast and shook the recipient to the core.

I'd personally witnessed Master Chen in action. I'd stood, neck craned, to see him wrap up his final class.

"Come," he said, indicating I step forward. He took my wrist and positioned my hand like a white-gloved traffic cop indicating 'stop!' "Make your stand," he said, stepping back.

I was barely positioned. Wham! Every bone in my little hand felt shattered? It was quick as a lightning bolt – I hadn't even seen him move. Now, that was power!

"Rooting," he said, "is everything. It is both a base and a

foundation. It is one of the most important things in life. A good building must have a strong and firm base. A successful company needs a good foundation. A healthy plant requires a healthy root. The excellent flow of Tai Chi Chuan movements must have a steady, firm root. Without a strong root, the whole body will not be able to relax."

Relaxation is the ultimate goal for all Tai Chi Chuan players. Soft, slow, gentle flowing movements require a strong and firm base in the foot. Once the foot is firm, the other parts of the body can move freely and stay relaxed. The foot's root itself should not be too relaxed or loose.

When the entire foot is rooted, the three points on the medial or inner aspect of the sole are of particular importance. The first point is the big toe; the other two points are on the inner part of the heel and the inner part of the ball of the foot. These points are on opposite sides of the instep. The Master calls these points "the three active nails."

When the foot is rooted, these three points grip like three nails penetrating the ground, but without the 'Tan Tien's' support, the nails remain inactive. Activation, lies with the mind to signal Tan Tien to connect – without connection – there is no rooting. With three active nails, strongly secured, the mind and body are relaxed. In turn, the peaceful mind loosens the joints, softens the muscles – then, all will open up. The root will continue to stay firm and sturdy.

Amber and I stood, facing each other, our bare feet firmly planted shoulder width apart. My left foot moved forward to align with the inside of Amber's right. Synchronised, arms, legs and torsos moved in all directions. Her eyes softly fell upon mine.

"Waxing – Waning – Pushing – Yielding," she repeated, again and again. Her rhythmic tone lulled our eyes closed as her voice fell to a silence.

And suddenly, I realised, she was showing me how it works, rather than simply telling me.

$$=><=$$

Minds and bodies back on track, it was time for our last supper.

"Hey, Kim – how'd ya go?" called Jimmy. He was accompanied by a rather large gent.

"Depends. Who's your friend?" I asked, reluctant to reveal all without an introduction to his companion.

"This ugly bugger?" he said with a suggestive look.

"Seamus," the man in question announced, taking my hand. He's a cracker, I thought, a big, broad, dark, stunning Irishman. To conceal my attraction, I goofed like Monkey. Jimmy roared with laughter, and I just made out Seamus ask, "What the heck?"

But then I wasn't goofing anymore. My nervous system was under attack – I couldn't stop my legs, they were quick stepping out of control. I felt the panic on my face as I fell to the ground, exhausted and shaking like a leaf. One eye saw black. I tried speaking, but for a moment I couldn't make a single comprehendible sound come out of my mouth.

"Go. Get help," Jimmy calmly told Seamus. "It's MS."

Soon, my shaking stilled but every nerve and sinew continued twitching. It felt like I'd been plugged into an electricity supply. Small shocks prickled the full length of my spine, down the back of my legs to my feet. I tried rubbing my limbs back to life but it was no use. My fingers were numb and my arms weak. My temperature rose with anger. I didn't like being unable to do things for myself – I felt hopeless. I didn't know how to ask for help. With a burst of pain, my eyes flooded. I'd never prayed before but in that moment I begged the Earth's Keepers to save me from the slippery slope.

"Here, you silly Monkey," said Jimmy, taking control. "Let me."

"Are you warm enough?" he asked, slipping his windcheater over his head. "Don't worry. You'll be fine; you've beaten it before and you'll beat it again. I know you!"

"I'm too hot" I replied, indicating I didn't need his top. "Would you put me in the shade, please?"

Jimmy gathered my hideous, pathetic body up in his arms. He carried my dead weight to the nearest tree and gently sat me on the grass so the trunk supported me.

"I know it's hard but try to relax," he said gently. "Help will be here soon."

"I am a silly Monkey, aren't I?" I laughed, trying to divert the conversation. "Do you really think I'm out of control?" I looked up at him to find his eyes fearful.

"What makes you ask?" Jimmy kept rubbing my arms and legs, trying to get them to work.

"Well. It just dawned on me. They say Tai Chi is life, or controlled energy in perpetual motion," I explained, wide eyed at the revelation. "But what then controls the energy?"

Had my nature kept me on the move? Or had I, like the Romans in search of gold, chosen to defy nature by commandeering its role? And like Pinocchio, with no strings to hold me down – was I a gypsy girl, out of control?

I suddenly realised I'd learned what I needed to know. Coria had shown me I had the power to actualise my dreams. First, I had to stop falling down and really connect. I needed to stay firm and sturdy – or as Master Chen put it, find my roots.

Now it was time to move on.

===><===

7
SOUTH AMERICA

I'd been thinking about Dougal a lot during my time at Coria. Almost two decades earlier in the Alice, I'd seen the joy in his face as he remembered travelling in Cancun and I'd known then that I would one day visit the Yucatan myself. It seemed particularly appropriate, then, that I begin my South American journey at the solitary beer hut he'd described by the light of the fire all those years ago. I'd imagined the solitary bar as a straw-capped Hawaiian-style number on beach-white, fine-grained sand – the kind you see in movies. The reality before me was completely different. The hut had survived the test of time but looked like it wouldn't last much longer. The same could be said for the bar stool that I tried to perch on awkwardly – I felt like I was teetering on the brink of a disaster.

The establishment's owner wasn't too flash either. I doubted he'd seen water since Dougal's visit. He didn't really look Mexican to me – in fact, he looked rather like a cross between Catweazle and Robinson Crusoe. He was tall and thin, with grey hair and a long scraggly beard that ended in a point – his skin was a dirty brown and his hair verging on yellow instead of

Catweazle grey. He might have been a Swede or a Dane, but under that layer of dirt, who knew? Anyway, he was an endearing, helpful character. He offered me a free, guided tour of the peninsula as he proceeded to drag a nicotine-stained finger around an old washed out map on the wall.

I sat sipping an ice cold San Miguel, watching him wipe his glasses with a dirty cloth, a rolled cigarette drooping lopsidedly from his lips, when I noticed something unexpected.

"Is that a computer you have back there?" I asked. I stumbled on my dismount from the rickety stool in my excitement.

"A temperamental one," he replied.

"How much to check my emails?" I returned, reaching for my wallet. I'd come straight from Coria and I hadn't had access to my inbox for an age.

He smiled coyly, his mouth a ravage of nicotine stained enamel tombstones.

"For pretty ladies, nothing," he said. I gulped, nodded and gingerly edged my way past him to the computer.

There was an email from Liz in Canada –

You've been on my mind a lot recently, Kim. I just heard from Charles – remember, my friend I insisted you should meet? The successful New Zealand real estate agent?
Well, I still believe, YOU'RE PERFECT FOR EACH OTHER!
He's in the UK. Will you meet with him?
Please. Pretty please.
Your dear friend – etc.

The stories she'd told me about Charles made him seem like a good fit for me. But, there, in a place where Dougal was very much on my mind, I wasn't really interested in a new partner. But I sent back an email to say I'd think about it. You never know what's around the corner and – after my resolutions in Spain – I was a firm believer in taking hold of opportunities with both hands as they presented themselves.

=><=

Cancun itself was of little interest. It wasn't the cute paradise I'd imagined, so I made my way through Mexico's Yucatan Peninsula, travelling east to west, stopping and staying as I pleased. Some villages offered no accommodation while others were fully occupied. I managed to get a bed each night and, more often than not, a reasonable meal. My hosts were extraordinarily special; always kind, generous and full of humour — and keen to sell. I fondly remembered Luca's words, "The world is the same all over. People are people, and we're fundamentally the same!"

One hot afternoon, I took a break with other tourists in a Mexico City café. As I sat with a cool drink in the corner, a couple of young girls entered with rag dolls tightly clutched in their tiny hands. Street children, I'd thought immediately. Then I took a closer look. Belying their forlorn expressions, they each had beautiful, crystal clear eyes, white teeth and what appeared to be pretty cotton dresses hanging below grubby, matted overcoats.

It soon became clear they routinely worked this café. I saw the waiter nod and smile at them before they systematically worked the tables – one to the left, the other to the right. In a moment they had sold all their dolls. Suddenly, the door swung open. An old woman launched through the doorway and with one swift swipe she grabbed the money from both girls. With another she forced a second batch of dolls into those tiny hands

– not a coin or a doll fell to the floor. The girls' eyes were terror-filled as the woman pushed them forcefully back inside the café. I couldn't believe it. Was the performance staged for the tourists' benefit? Or had I just experienced a real, live, Oliver Twist scenario? Like Fagan, had the old woman traded conscience for the pursuit of wealth?

I had the totally opposite experience when I was looking for somewhere to sleep later that day. I was following some hastily given directions to my request for good, affordable lodgings from a shopkeeper but I really didn't know where I was going. Nevertheless, I walked briskly down ramshackle streets to make it look like I had purpose – I didn't want anyone to think I had no clue where I was going and therefore open myself up to interference. From the shopkeeper's description in halting English, I had imagined a small, single storey, dirty white house with warm, welcoming lights shining through the timber framed windows, set either side of the front door.

From a distance I spotted the house just as I'd envisioned – except there were no welcome lights. To be precise, there were no windows and seemingly no front door. I turned sideways to squeeze through the hedge, a miniscule gap of unyielding brambles. With my newly rediscovered Tai Chi precision, I consciously planted one foot on the uneven dirt track through the unkempt jungle of a garden that lead to the door, before shifting my weight to the other. It didn't feel right – a shiver went up my spine – but it was too late to turn back. I was committed. And it was almost dark.

The door opened as if by magic as I raised my hand to knock.

"Hello. Hello. Anyone there?" I called nervously. I waited. When no one appeared, I cautiously stepped forward to peek behind the door.

Suddenly, an old man's wizened face appeared very close at

chest height. Shocked and shaking, I jumped back, breathing heavily. I wanted to run but my feet wouldn't move.

"Room?" said the face, without raising an eye.

"Yes?" I managed to squeak, putting a more comfortable distance between us. Who answers a door like that? I wondered. Should I run now? "Never agree to do things you don't want to," I remembered from my Bali trip but, before I could retreat, another wizened character appeared – a lady. His wife? Strangely, I no longer felt as terrified – perhaps they were just as wary of the foreigner on their doorstep as she was of them?

Trying to shake the feeling something sinister was lurking beneath the surface, I followed the beam of light they were shining towards a small outhouse, barely visible out the back. Was that to be my room for the night? They offered me no words, just wiggled the flashlight to indicate I walk ahead. I took each step gingerly – nervous that I couldn't see the odd couple behind me. I cursed my active imagination – was I being kidnapped? Would anyone ever find me? Who would even notice I'd gone missing?

I pushed open the door – four walls, no windows, a straw roof of sorts and a floor made from packed earth. I just made out a bed, squidgy, lumpy and damp looking. I plonked down on the edge of it. Yep, damp. It was going to be a long, long night.

The couple shut the door leaving me in the half dark. I dared not move. I was already convinced every bug in the world lived in that mattress. I heard mice – or rats – scurrying somewhere nearby, which explained the horrendous smell. Why had I not run away when I'd had the chance?

I laughed out loud, mostly to appease my fears. Personal porter? No chance. Gold nuggets? Nup. Beautiful, wafting fragrances – not a hope in hell! Which tourist board needed to hear of this place?

The rattle of the door pricked my nerves. I held my breath

then expelled it in relief as I saw a young girl enter my cell, followed by the old lady carrying a kerosene lamp.

"Are you alright? You don't look at all well," the girl asked in fluent English.

"Er, fine… thank you," I gulped faintly waiting to discover what fresh hell lay before me.

"I'm Greta. Would you like some tea?" she asked as she placed the tray beside my bed.

'You must be kidding – I'm not drinking anything here,' I thought.

"Oh, yes please," my cursed good English manners replied as I reached politely for the tray she held. Moving closer I saw she was seriously pretty, her glossy, almost black hair hanging long and straight to her waist. She had fine features and long lashes, enhanced by silky, pale chocolate skin that glowed under the kerosene lamp.

"Greta, may I ask after the old couple? I don't understand why, but it feels something's terribly wrong," I said, "Are they alright?"

"That's very perceptive of you," she said. "My grandparents – they live in fear of evil. Just after I was born my mother was taken. The whole community searched for years. Everyone said she'd be fine – but she never returned."

"One day a man came knocking, claiming to know what happened to her." Greta continued. "I don't know how much you know about Mayan mythology, but the man told my grandparents a story to chill their bones. They haven't really recovered."

"He said they were the direct descendants of two brothers, banished to the underworld," she went on as I listened, alarmed yet fascinated. "It's said my grandfather's lineage carries the burden of his ancestor, Vacub, who agreed to sacrifice his life for the sake of his brother Hun. But Vacub reneged and the underworld wanted revenge."

"Throughout the centuries, the first-born male of each generation has paid Vacub's price. My grandfather, second-born in his family, lost his sight protecting his elder brother from his fate. He's been living in fear of evil forces ever since – he believes they'll soon come knocking."

"He was caught unprepared when you came. He's so embarrassed for the way he greeted you – please forgive him. He's a frightened old man. You see, I'm the first, and only child born in the line of my grandfather's brother, like my mother before me," Greta explained. "Grandpa believes they'll come for me, too."

She saw the startled look on my face.

"Oh, please don't worry for me," she said, "I'm not a believer! If you want to know more, I recommend Uxmal," Greta said then bade me good night.

=><=

The huge, grey stone pyramid at Uxmal was fascinating, the first I'd ever seen, let alone climbed. It was discovered covered in weeds in the middle of an ancient forest — the excavators had also found a swastika cloth at its epicentre. I was bemused when I read about it — I'd only known the swastika as a Nazi insignia.

I fell in with a tour group where I met Alison, an English lady travelling with her two young children.

"Are you going to the top of the pyramid?" She asked after we'd had a brief, general conversation. I nodded.

"Would you mind taking my children up? Just to keep an eye on them really, they're well-behaved," she requested, adding: "I can't go up. I'm not well enough. I've got cancer."

I was willing but a little hesitant, too. I didn't know much about children. Whenever the subject of them came up I'd been uncertain whether I wanted any. With the MS diagnosis the topic had come up again, but I too busy reeling from shock to seriously consider the issue. There's a time and place, and it wasn't then. I'd had enough to contend with.

"You should have children! You'd make a great mum. I'll be a surrogate for you if you need it," my sister said, out of the blue. I was dumbstruck. She'd never expressed an interest in parenting, quite the opposite really. And my life had hardly presented adequately stable conditions for having children, let alone raising them. Plus the fact there was no father on the horizon and I certainly hadn't considered being a single parent, by design.

So it was with some trepidation that I followed the two rug rats up the pyramid's steep stairs. There was little chance of me keeping an eye on them – I'd barely answered in the affirmative when the little 'delights' were off like rockets. When we reached the top I saw their mum waiting nervously with icy poles in hand; so I coaxed them back down and back into her tender care.

As they greedily sucked on their ice creams, Alison told me about their trip. She was introducing her children to the world of travel, creating lasting memories for them because she wouldn't be able to later — her cancer was terminal.

They'd gone from England to Africa for a lightning tour of the north, south and Egypt, where they had more time to explore the ancient sites. By mid-May they'd arrived in Australia with a phenomenal to-do list, flying between destinations to ensure the most time for activities and attractions before a quick stop over in Japan and then onto New Zealand. In early July, they'd touched down in South America to work their way north to the Yucatan Peninsula.

Their trip would continue north, stopping, first in the Galapagos Islands, then on through the United States into Canada before returning home for the new school year. I felt incredibly sad for them but also great joy because they were sharing such wonderful family times. If I'm honest, there was also a pang of jealousy – I wished I had someone who cared that much about me. I wondered what it would be like to have a fellow journeyman. I'd frequently encountered couples travelling before tying the knot. Many said, "If we survive this trip, we'll survive marriage." The words never failed to amuse me – surely marriage must be a darn sight harder than travel? But what would I know?

We stood looking down at The Grand Ball Court. One hundred and forty-six metres by thirty-seven, with two parallel eight metres high stone walls, flanked the flat ninety-five-metres-long rectangular play area. Set high into the wall on each side were large vertical stone markers — rings carved with intertwined feathered serpents. Some markers had a quatrefoil cartouche indicating the entrance to the underworld — experts speculate the game may have symbolised the movement of the sun (the ball) through the underworld (the court) each night. Alternatively, the ball may have represented another heavenly body such as the moon with the court symbolising the world. Sculpted panels on the sloping base walls depicted players — one, decapitated, emitted streams of blood in the form of wriggling snakes.

The exact rules of the game still remain unknown, but in all probability there would have been variations by culture and era. The objective was to get a solid latex rubber ball (they'd found some remarkably preserved in the bogs of El Manatí. They were 10 to 30 cm in diameter, weighing five hundred grams to three and a half kilograms — a weapon in itself), through one of the rings using only your elbows, knees, thighs and shoulders — no hands. Some games allowed the use of sticks. Remarkably, preserved balls had been found in the mud nearby.

Players were both professional and amateur, but warriors and war captives were often forced to entertain. Decorated courts show players wore protective gear such as belts, padding for the knees, hips, elbows and wrists — some even wore grilled helmets, guards and gauntlets. It sounded like a forerunner to

American Football. Winners' trophies — hachas and palma, a human head, arm, hand, a player or a fan-tailed bird, as well as other carved stones items — were buried with them as a link between the sport and the underworld in Mesoamerican mythology.

But although winners were celebrated – just like today – their popularity was a world away from today's bling-ed out football heroes. Religiously significant, the captain or the whole team was often beheaded as a sacrifice to the gods. In fact, a relief at Chichén Itzá shows two teams of seven players decapitated and the classic Mayans were known to run a parallel game — the once defeated captives were tied into balls and then unceremoniously rolled down the stone steps from the platform where we were seated. Can you imagine football celebrities putting up with that today?

The Mayan's game was invented sometime in the Preclassical Period (2500-100 BCE), and spread quickly throughout Mesoamerica. Mythology played an important part: particularly the story of the Mayan gods Hun Hunahpú and Vucub Hunahpú. Yes, the two brothers Greta had supposedly been descended from! I listened carefully as the tour guide told the story. The gods of the underworld, annoyed by the brothers' noisy playing, tricked them into descending into Xibalba (the underworld) where they were challenged to a ball game. The loser would have his head cut off, setting a precedent for future games in the world above ground. Vacub bravely agreed to lose and save his brother's life. However, when it came to it, he must have felt the sacrifice too great – who wouldn't? He won the game and Hun Hunahpús lost his life instead.

It was interesting, but I remained unconvinced. It was just a myth – and someone had rather nastily invoked it to explain Greta's mother's disappearance. Throughout the ages, every culture has told stories to explain their beliefs or natural phenomena. And, over time, some of those stories become myths – symbolic representations of our inner psyches that ultimately became signposts on an inner journey of meaning and discovery. In fact, I knew the word 'myth' came from the Greek mythos, which simply meant story. Stories existed long before art, language or the written word – even before religion, whose stories retold universal mythical themes – the creation of the world, the first man and woman, heaven and earth. Combine myth and humanity's capacity for imagination and you get great literary works; Noah's Ark, Jonah and the Whale, Moby Dick and even Titanic hold their sway over the popular imagination because, at their heart, they're based on earlier myths of our struggle against nature.

At its simplest, myths address fundamental, difficult questions we seek to answer, in making sense of things. We find ourselves in this strange, dangerous world, over which we have very little control. We want to know, the machinations of the universe – What is it? How and where did it all begin? But, most of all we seek to understand - Who and what am I? Where did I come from? Why am I here? How should I live? What should I to do? We ask, why there is 'something' rather than 'nothing'. Although, myths are generally exaggerated and understood to be fictitious, they are by definition, true – they're an embodiment of our beliefs, concepts and a way to question - to make sense of the world.

Listening to the tale of the two brothers, I realised the seeds of mythical stories run deep and across generations, where they can be powerful instigators of cultural change or stagnation. I thought of Greta's grandfather's eye. He'd virtually imprisoned himself for fear of the mythological underworld. Would his fear be passed down to his granddaughter… and her granddaughter? Or would Greta break the cycle?

For that matter, what were my own personal myths – and was I allowing myself to be imprisoned or liberated by the stories that shaped my life?

I was suddenly transported back to the afternoon I'd spent at William Rickets sanctuary all those years ago with my grandparents. I thought I'd felt the earth eyes on me then, rather like the eyes in the back of my mothers' head when she'd keep us in line. I'd believed the earths' keepers had been watching – they'd kept me in check. As I'd grown up, I'd felt their presence wax and wane, push, pull, stop, start and challenge my every turn, every decision I'd made. But were they my puppeteers or did I pull my own strings?

$$= > < =$$

In an old Merida convent, I accessed my inbox for the first time in weeks and was surprised to find an email from Charles.

> Hi Kim,
> Apologies for brevity, Liz gave me your details.
> I'm in the UK wondering whether it would be possible to meet sometime over the next twenty-four hours — I'm booked on a return flight to New Zealand tomorrow.
> Hope to hear by return.
> Chogs.

I bashed out a quick response.

> Hi Charles.
> Sorry, impossible – I'm in South America. Another time, maybe?
> Shame!

I signed off a little sarcastically, but in truth, I was a tad disappointed. I'd been considering meeting him – there's nothing like travelling on your own to make you feel like connecting with another person.

= > < =

The accommodation was better than expected at the old nunnery, a little more than basic, quiet and pristine. I took a quick shower then headed to the main square. It was early evening and the joint was jumping. It didn't appear to be a special occasion but it felt as if the whole town was out for the night — dancers performing the salsa, flamenco, merengue, cha-cha and others dances I didn't know by name, musicians with guitars, vihuelas, violins and percussion, and traditionally dressed mothers accompanying the pretty chicas and handsome chicos who offered tapas treats as they sauntered.

I had a ball. My foot hadn't even touched the square before I held a round paper plate laden with delicious looking food in one hand and a folded paper serviette, plastic fork and spoon in the other. 'Wow, my kinda place', I thought as a dumpy lady shuffled me to a white plastic garden chair. I'd come alive in an instant. Before I knew it, I'd been roped into help – I repositioned the white plastic garden chairs, ran fresh food from the vans to the stalls and even prepared some salsa. People arrived. More food arrived. And beautiful, some not so, men swept me off my feet. I just loved to dance – the music, movement and men – set me free. I was alive.

I could quite easily have made Merida home. I'd felt a part of the community, the minute I stepped out the nunnery door. There must have been something in the air. It was as though I'd lived there all my life.

Waiting for a flight from Mexico City to Lima, I was surprised to find another email from Charles at the airport.

Hi Kim,
With regret – We were unable to connect, in the UK.
Short notice – I know. Sorry.
Our mutual friend, Liz told me all about you. I've known

her, and her ex, for a long time. Was most perturbed
when they split. I was in NZ. Unable to offer support –
she's a terrific woman. Apparently, you are too?
Don't know what you know of me. But I know Liz. I
suspect you know the size of my underpants! And, none
of it true. Joking.
FYI – I'm six feet something. Well built. Hazel eyes. Fair
– hair and complexion. Attached photo will confirm.
Please. Keep me posted on your travels.
Chogs.

I still had no romantic notions but was pleasantly surprised
when I opened the attachment to see the unsolicited photograph
(of course, this was long before the days of social media). There
was Charles in an old fashioned bathtub, cowboy boots sticking
out one end, an Akubra at the other and a hand gripping a stubby
somewhere about the middle — set in the middle of a field! He
looked like he might be tall and the mop on top of his head was
very fair. Nice but not my type – I was more into short, dark and
swarthy.

I waited till I arrived in Arequipa to reply.

Hi Charles,
Apologies for delayed reply. Travel messes with your
timing.
Thanks for your newsy email and photo. Highly
amusing.
Here's a snapshot of what I've been up to:
Arrived in Lima. Explored museums, catacombs and
street markets. Encountered both wealthy and the poorest
of poor. Strange.
Against better judgement joined an organised tour to Port
Maldonado in the Amazon. Luckily only a handful of
travellers who got on quite well, mostly.

Travelled up river to a hideout — traditional huts
surrounded by amazing flora and fauna and a crazy
Toucan that wiled away time biting through toes of
tourists' sneakers.
Travelled through jungle. Bought new sneakers. Visited
umpteen towns celebrating some festival or another –
right time of year to be on the road here.
Now, I'm in Arequipa, or "La blanca cuidad" (the white
city). Unbelievably beautiful architecture. Sat in the
Plaza de Armas drinking beer and Pisco Sours
(refreshing cocktail of Peruvian pisco, lime juice, syrup,
ice, egg white and angostura bitters) watching a never-
ending parade perform and dance in traditional dress.
Tomorrow it's the Catalina Monastery then a look at the
Ice Maiden, Momia Juanita. Will write from Cuzco in a
few weeks, before Inca Trails trek.
Hope you enjoy my travelogue.
Be well.
Kim

=><=

The Santa Catalina Monastery was most impressive, a city
within a city. Time was short but a couple of us just made it in to
see Momia Juanita, the 500-year-old sacrificial girl. The 13-year-
old mummified girl is also known as the Inca Ice Maiden and
Lady of Ampato, after Mt. Ampato in the Peruvian Andes where
she was discovered. The hot ash of a nearby volcanic eruption,
over 500 years ago, had slowly melted the snow and ice over to
reveal a brightly coloured burial tapestry, an aksu — and Juanita.
The sacrifice, or capacocha, would have been made to appease
the mountain god who was the protector and controller of natural
forces that ensured sufficient rain, crops and livestock and kept
order amongst the Inca people. Sacrifices often coincided with

auspicious events, such as the death of an emperor, earthquakes, eclipses and droughts. Offerings were made from the highest point that could be reached — the ice-clad summits.

It took incredible effort to hold sacrificial rituals in the thin air and life threatening cold of the high Andes. Johan Reinhard, the anthropologist who discovered Juanita at 20,000 feet, also discovered evidence of substantial Inca camps or 'rest stops' enroute and at the summit. They were made of wood, stone and dried grasses, materials that would have taken great effort to haul miles up the barren mountainside in the high altitude's thin air. The trek to the sacrificial site was itself a remarkable undertaking — an entourage of hundreds of llamas and porters from the village had to carry provisions, water and symbolic, ritualistic paraphernalia with them. Juan de Betanzos wrote of widespread child sacrifices, up to thousands, according to the testimony of his wife — who had been married to Atahualpa, an Incan Emperor.

Naturally mummified in a huddled foetal position, as if to keep warm, Juanita's hair was plaited in more than a hundred braids and miniature idols and keepsakes surrounded her in her tomb of ice. She was first thought to be of a noble family because she was found dressed in the finest Cuzco textiles and of a portly physique. However, biochemical analysis suggests something more unpalatable. Her braided locks revealed a diet of controlled substances like coca and chicha, a fermented brew of maize during the last two years of her life. Evidence supports historical accounts that children who were selected to take part in sacred ceremonies each year showed changes in their hair due to their food, coca, and alcohol consumption. These changes ultimately marked their intended sacrifice.

Chronicles suggest a maiden was chosen at puberty to live under the guidance of a priestess. In selection for sacrifice, one year prior to her actual death her life dramatically changed, as did her surging consumption of coca and alcohol. In sacrificial circumstances, coca and alcohol disoriented and sedated young victims to make them readily accept their own gruesome fate. Evidence has shown that, during her last year of life, she consumed elite foods — maize and animal protein, perhaps llama meat. Her body recorded high levels of coca, And there was an alcohol surge in her last six to eight weeks to help her enter a higher altered state — the final build-up to capacocha. Then, on the sacrificial day, she was likely put into a stupor or even rendered unconscious.

I chewed on the realisation that young Greta, born in another time, could have suffered Juanita's fate. Looking at her skeleton, imagining the petite, fine-boned child, I thought how lucky Greta was to have a grandfather who loved her so dearly he would exchange his life for hers. What might have become of Juanita, had someone done the same for her – what kind of life might she have lived? And I couldn't help but wonder whether my life might have been different if I'd followed my parents' lead, instead of always choosing an alternative path? Would I now have a permanent home somewhere, with someone with whom I belonged? What had I sacrificed by doing everything my way?

=><=

Hi Charles,
I gazed on a 500-year-old little girl today. It made me feel privileged, but weird – I felt lifeless, yet deeply connected. It was as if her soul communicated with mine – no words, nor images. A sentiment I'll never forget – so empty. But comforted.
There she was, encased in her temperature-controlled, transparent cube in the small air-conditioned room of the

Museum of Andean Sanctuaries. Silent, demure and respectful, she had a chilling story to tell.

That poor wee lassie - she never had a chance. No choices. No options. Groomed for sacrificial purpose. Relaxed in her seated position amongst untouched artefacts and her undisturbed feathered headdress, she looks like she just drifted into death, chewing the coca leaves found in her mouth.

Sometimes I wonder…

Afterwards I ate a swamp river rat. It tasted pretty much as you'd expect. Chewy. Don't ask.

Inca trails next. Will write again after.

Kim.

=><=

Cuzco and its surrounds were everything I'd imagined and more. A hub for exploring the Peruvian Andes, its complex past and beautiful legends, the town is amazing — an amalgam of an Inca capital and colonial city authentically presented in its original layout with a remarkable architectural heritage, festivals, arts, tiny streets, and squares with stunning fountains.

Incan mythology attributes the foundation of the City of Cuzco to Manco Cápac. Tradition says the golden sceptre, given to Cápac by the Sun, was thrust into Cuzco's fertile soil to designate a place for the Incan capital. Over fifty-five years, two great leaders and 50,000 men built their ideal city according to an extremely hierarchical organisation. There were spaces for religious, economic and administrative functions, rivers turned into canals to prevent frequent flooding, and satellite towns featuring cultivated zones for agricultural, artisanal, and industrial production.

Perched on a dilapidated stone wall, I paused to reflect on the magnificent city and its cathedral below. From the moment

I'd arrived in Cuzco, I'd felt special – blessed. It wasn't a place I'd hankered to see. Quite the opposite, in fact – too many people talked of 'doing the Inca Trail', which tended to put me off. But, as I sat alone with my thoughts I became more captivated by what I'd seen and learned. Fifty years in the making, the cathedral astounded me not so much by its architecture – which was nevertheless impressive – but by the townfolk's commitment and service to realising their dream. Together, 50,000 men had cooperated to achieve a single purpose. I was familiar with the expression, "Rome wasn't built in a day," but I don't think it was until I sat there high above Cuzco that I'd finally understood what that meant – success comes with knowing your purpose, and sticking with it.

A friend once gave me a wee book.

"I'm sorry if you don't like this," she'd said, "I was inspired to buy it for you."

It was a beautiful pocket sized hardback with a simple design and illustrations. Inside, there were only a few words per page but my attention had been gripped by just one page. It said:

'Don't get creative after you've made a decision.'

In other words, creativity has no meaning when it lacks purpose. And that was my problem, I realised. I'd not lacked creativity in planning my life. I was full of inspiration about what I should do next. I just lacked the strong sense of direction and purpose that would give my journey meaning.

Rather than hit the town on my last night, I opted for a long hot bath to rest my tired feet, then nestled into a well-deserved comfortable bed with an award-winning wine I'd purchased from a cellar door in the Maipo Valley. Beyond my window was an open expanse of vines dressed with a rose bush at either end; the colours, mist and smells ignited fond memories of running through an Australian vineyard as a teenager.

There was a knock followed by an envelope thrust underneath my door.

140 | THE GAP

I picked up the crisp envelope with beautiful calligraphy bearing my name and the hotel's address. It was postmarked New Zealand. Inside I found an invitation to witness the world's first glimpse of the new millennium at Gisborne.

Charles was having a party and I was invited.

8

NEW ZEALAND

I was woken by the grinding of landing wheels being released. For a moment I'd forgotten where I was – which country was I touching down in now? Then, suddenly remembering, a wave of apprehension swept over me. It felt like my temperature had risen a degree or two.

"This is for real," I murmured to myself. It was all well and good falling for this guy online, but how would it work in the real world? Somehow I'd never questioned I was travelling half way around the world for what was essentially a blind date. Now that I was here, it was a bit late to get cold feet.

Moonlight

Just before Christmas I'd hopped a flight from Santiago to Auckland on spec. Weak in body, fuzzy in head, I was transferred to one of those jet propelled pencil planes that reminded me of a childhood game, the one where you wound rubber bands around pencils then released them in hope of hitting someone. I just wanted to sleep.

I let out a long deep breath as we taxied to the tiny terminal.

Everything would be just fine. After all, Charles had come recommended by one of my most reliable friends.

Gisborne Airport was just what you'd expect in a rural community in the middle of nowhere: a solo concrete runway and a terminal more like a small bungalow. The propellers stilled. The steps were secured. Alighting no more than a few paces from the building, I was shocked as someone HUGE stepped forward to hug me.

"Hello! Please hold this," I stuttered and made a dash for a pee — not that I needed one. But I had to gather my thoughts.

"What! Not even a hug?" I heard Charles call as I ran.

Not bloody likely, I thought.

He was tall, as expected, but the well-built man in the photo he'd sent me had turned to podge. At first glance he appeared to be a big pappy ogre – a real live 'Shrek'. He seemed gentle as in the photograph, when I'd thought he might be my kind of guy. Now, other than the colour of his eyes, skin and hair, there was little resemblance. The healthy young chappie with bright, bold features full of life had virtually disappeared. His eyes were barely visible – they'd been swallowed whole like pissholes in the snow of his puffy features. He had cauliflower ears. His nose was deeply pitted and bulbous, while his lips… would definitely not be touching mine!

In that instant before I made a mad run for the loo, I'd felt he'd shamelessly deceived me.

Taking a few deep breaths in the bathroom, splashing some water on my face, and giving myself a good talking to, I made my way back to Charles, who'd lugged my bags into the terminal. To avoid eye contact, I looked him up and down. Here I'd travelled half way around the world to meet him and he'd clearly made no effort to create a good first impression in his dirty, frayed t-shirt and scruffy shorts.

"Nice to see you dressed for the occasion," I said with disdain.

You can tell a lot about a person's state of mind by how they take care of themselves and their possessions. My bad premonition on the flight reached a fever pitch as we approached Charles's black four-by-four – it was covered in old dust and cobwebs, the glass so filthy I couldn't see through it. Like a gent he opened the door for me; I swept old food boxes off the seat into the footwell to squeeze myself in. I winced as my feet crunched on a pile of rubbish when I slid into the cabin.

Stop being so critical, I berated myself. Don't judge a book and all that.

Unable to contain himself, Charles jabbered non-stop. I had no idea what he said as my foggy head worsened and my stomach churned. I couldn't determine whether I was sick from travel or sick of him – already? He appeared to be on a mission.

"We're going to a garden party!" He informed me. "My neighbour's a film producer, he's followed our story every step of the way. He thinks he'll make a movie if things turn out well between us."

"Mmm," I grunted. I felt too sick to respond.

"It's exciting don't you think?" he asked, not really wanting an answer. "I thought we should go away for a few days, to get to know each other before my other five guests arrive?"

Garden parties. Other guests. Bloody hell! I was sure his plans were well intentioned, but I felt absolutely awful. He seemed to have no consideration for the fact I'd just got off a long-haul flight – all he wanted was for us to party.

No way, Jose, I said to myself. At least get me in the house first.

I soon regretted the thought. Liz had said his house was something quite special and it was. Not grand, but with that sense of history and character I so like in a building. I bent to untie my shoelaces in the entrance hall, the honey coloured timber panelling beautiful under the atmospheric-hued lights he'd left on for extra charm. Next to me, he pulled off one ugly, cumbersome baseball shoe using his other foot on the back of the shoe — it was a pet hate, the epitome of laziness in my book.

My energy plummeted. From our correspondence, I'd expected a man of substance, presence and panache. Instead I was left wondering how I would survive a week in his presence.

"Come with me," Charles said, attempting to take me by the hand, "I'll take you to your room. And then we'll see what remedies I have."

An out of the way, narrow staircase took us to the upper level. It was a delightful room – light, bright and sparsely furnished, pleasantly decked out with quaint, old-fashioned floral printed linen, kind of like a trendy old lady's house. The double bed was conveniently placed to access the en-suite and enjoy the treetop view. 'A wee place to hide from the ogre,' I thought with glee.

"Which side do you prefer?" he asked, opening the window.

"If you think I'm sharing your bed you've got another thing coming, sunshine!" I blurted without thinking. I was mortified that he would take the liberty.

The look on his face was priceless.

"What the hell made you think I was going to hop into bed with you?" I said, not wanting a response – I wasn't up for an argument.

"Your emails," he replied. "They were all lovey dovey. I assumed you'd fallen in love with me."

"You can't be serious!" I said in no uncertain term. "You've clearly been dreaming."

"So what did you come all this way for?" He asked all innocent.

"Charles. You were very kind to invite me but, lets face it, what chance was there really of any 'nice' girl hopping straight into bed with you?" I said, trying to calm a potentially inflammatory situation.

"What I mean is, I've been on the go for days, I'm sick and I just can't imagine having to share a bed anytime soon. I need time and space to get better. Let's go to your friends and see what tomorrow brings?" I suggested.

"Okay, but we're not done yet," he said stepping forward to give me a hug. "No time to unpack – we're expected down the road."

Plied with Echinacea and other herbal remedies, I took the short walk through a neighbourhood that screamed 'old money' so Charles could parade me in front of his neighbours. The street was picturesque with large, but not ostentatious, timber and brick houses. Sweetly refreshing tropical scents wafted from behind the low-rise walls and pruned hedges of manicured gardens. The equidistant trees had long, thin, delicate leaves that caught the summer sun as they shimmered in the breeze. They made me smile.

The minute we'd reached the driveway Charles took off down the side of the house and disappeared. I followed his path slowly, finding myself in an expansive backyard filled with people. Charles was nowhere to be seen but I fancied I could hear his voice in the distance somewhere.

"Welcome," a woman greeted me with an encouragingly friendly smile. "You must be Charles's friend. I'm Susie; it's my party. Come and we'll get you a drink." Strikingly tall and elegant, her long blonde hair was swept from her face and hooked behind one ear.

"You must be exhausted!" she exclaimed. "But where's Charles got to?" I gestured vaguely down towards the end of the garden.

"Ah! He must have joined Rob, my husband, and the others at the waterfront," Susie said. "We can join them if you like." She took one look at my face and added: "Or not – you do look tired."

"Thank you, Susie," I said hastily and gratefully. "If you really don't mind, I'm not feeling at all well."

"What was that man thinking?" Susie tisked, giving me a hug. "Here, have a drink then I'll find you a bed upstairs to nap."

I'd just ensconced myself in a delightfully soft padded armchair with a glass of wine in hand and was getting to know Susie better when Charles approached.

"Come on!" he said urgently. "We've got to get away before the traffic."

"Away? Away where?" asked Susie, echoing my words and aggravation exactly.

"I've got guests arriving. We're headed off for a few days to get to know each other without prying eyes," he replied in a hurried, excited voice.

"You're what? This girl needs rest – she's clearly unwell," Susie reprimanded. Charles looked at me briefly then looked away.

"I thought I'd show Kim Taupo's volcanic zone. She likes national parks and lots to see, do and learn – and I'm betting she'll love the forest's thermal pools and mountain."

'I'm right here, buddy,' I thought. 'No need to talk over me.'

"Anyway, I gave her Echinacea – that'll do the trick," said Charles, dismissively.

Looking apologetically at Susie, I dragged myself from the chair. I was too tired to argue. At least I might get some shut-eye on the road trip.

But my body had other plans. Although I wasn't in the mood for conversation — polite or otherwise – Charles managed to keep up the patter all the way to Taupo. Leaning my head against the window of his car, I rested wearily, feeling sorry for my sore head and myself. He passed me a map so I could track our progress. Mostly oblivious to my surrounds, I fought to keep my eyes open. I fleetingly remember a delightful, sky blue lake, but that was about it until we pulled up in front of our accommodation.

The 'hotel' turned out to be motel – a two storey, moss

stained, dark grey block that was hideously ugly. It must have been the worst building in Taupo.

"Up the stairs, turn left and you'll find your room, facing front — waterside," the concierge instructed.

Squeezed between two commercial buildings, the external stairway and balustrade had rusted through in places – I wasn't prepared to risk it taking Charles's weight as well as mine so on the third step I made out I'd left something in the car and sent him for it.

Waiting on the top landing for him to return with the key, my spirits lifted a little. This was a town I could really fall in love with. The breathtaking scenery was beyond anything I'd seen yet in my travels – it looked like nature's ultimate playground.

Charles opened the door, stepping aside to let me pass.

"I trust it's to your liking, Madam," he said, with a smile of delight.

My heart sunk as I took in the jacuzzi and double bed placed centre stage. Again, I couldn't believe he'd been so presumptuous! Flummoxed, I dropped my bag and lurched headlong for the balcony. Squeezing sideways past the bed, I drew back the flimsy cotton window covering. Relief! A gentle breeze gave me a small respite while I tried in vain to find the right words.

I'd wanted to shout, to throw a tantrum, and yell "What's wrong with you? Who the hell do you think I am?" I wanted to shake him awake – such a disrespectful ignoramus. But I'd never said such things before – so I didn't know how to now. I didn't have it in me. Anyway, even if I had mustered some gumption, I was too exhausted.

All I could think was I needed to sleep.

When I turned back he was sitting like a child on the bed flicking through local tourist magazines.

"What would you like for dinner?" he asked, not looking up.

Dinner was the furthest thing from my mind. I just wanted him to go away.

"How about room service? No, we should go out!" he exclaimed, before I could draw breath.

"Charles. Why don't you get it? I'm feeling just awful," I said as peevishly as possible. "Perhaps if I can take a nap now I'll be up to an outing later."

"But there's so much to see!" he replied, disappointed.

"Even so," I said. "Why don't you give me an hour by myself. Then we'll see."

=><=

It was cold and dark when Charles woke me, standing beside the bed holding a platter of food, piled high. Fresh crispy salad with fetta, grilled lamb cutlets, prawns and sardines. There was even a greasy spoon-style fish and chips plate covered in copious amounts of curry sauce and vermicelli noodles as a side. Don't get me wrong – I like each dish separately. But not together! And not now!

"Hello, sleepy head. I bought this for you. I've already eaten," he smirked.

I'd been out for hours. Feeling groggy, I didn't want to move. The smell of the food assaulted me. I wanted to throw up on him.

"Thanks but just...no," I croaked, barely able to muster a sentence, waving the plate away. My head was pulsing. My body ached. I felt hot and prickly.

"Look, there's not much point in being here if you don't get up and come out," he said snippily.

"Yes. I know. In my defence, I'm feeling utterly exhausted and sick," I looked up at him, hoping for a little compassion. No such luck.

"Don't worry. There's time. The bars are still open," he said, whipping back the bed sheet.

I didn't want to appear unappreciative or rude. He'd gone to some trouble to plan this getaway, even if I was less than impressed. And I felt reliant on him – I was sick and in a strange country where I knew no one. To be honest, I wasn't sure whether I completely knew where I was. So I dragged myself out of bed and made myself presentable.

We set off at too brisk a pace; I couldn't keep up. And that was saying something. He was hardly a fit and healthy specimen.

"Please can you slow down, Charles," I called.

"What's your tipple? I'll go ahead and get the drink in," he replied and shot off ahead without a glance back at me.

I continued at a snails pace along the wide street, barely a soul in sight. I turned the corner into a narrow, packed pedestrian precinct and suddenly there were crowds of people. Above their heads were old fashioned Victorian curved metal verandas, just like the ones in the old outlaw movies. Where the hell was Charles? I wanted to turn around and head straight back to the room. Music blared as voices raised trying to be heard over the racket.

"Kim, over here," a booming voice yelled. I considered pretending I hadn't seen the huge lump, by the bar flapping his arms above his head. I asked the Earth's Keepers to swallow me where I stood.

"What kept you?" he asked, handing me a glass of something bright and multi-coloured with a pink parasol and a cherry on stick. "I thought this pretty cocktail would put some colour back into your attitude." Charming.

"Ah! Sorry," I yelped as I let it slip through my fingers. It ran all down his pants.

"You!" He clearly had just stopped himself short of swearing at me. "Are you just trying to embarrass me?"

"Let's go somewhere else!" He continued, grabbing my hand to leave.

My head was pounding, my stomach growling and I was just not in the mood.

"This one!" he said, dragging me into a bar.

"No! It's too crowded and noisy," I said. "Charles, I'll wait out here."

He looked daggers at me. "I'll get you a seat and you'll be fine," he insisted.

I had no energy to argue. He stood facing me as I sat by the bar, head propped in my hands. Thankfully his big belly kept some space between us.

"You are so selfish!" Charles said. "Why don't you cheer up so we can relax and have a great time?"

I left him there and walked back to the hotel alone.

$$=><=$$

It was a beautiful morning. Except I was waking up next to Charles or, should I say, in the same bed as Charles. I'd spent the whole night hugging the edge of the bed. If I'd put any more distance between us I'd have been on the floor but what little sleep I got had gone a long way to reviving me and I was looking forward to a day of gentle activity exploring the great outdoors.

Charles was up for having breakfast out. Actually, that's an understatement. We could have fed an army with what he scoffed at the sidewalk breakfast bar. I asked if he had any plans for us, what we'd do for the day?

"It's almost lunch time," he grunted as he scraped the last morsel from his second breakfast plate. I almost fell off my chair.

"Well I'm going for a walk first," I said, leaving the table. Disappointed and alone, I strolled along the edge of a nearby lake. Johnny Cash's Folsom Prison was playing in my head. I figured I had two choices – stick with it and get back to Gisborne, or cross the line and find my own way. In that moment, I felt happy to do either but decided it wouldn't be fair to my host. For the moment I'd walk the line with Charles. For now.

"What a sensational day!" I called to some fishermen. "What's for dinner today, then?"

"Come see," they laughed.

I've loved fishing since the day I stopped, at the River Nene, to enquire why the bank was lined with anglers.

"What's going on?" I asked.

"There's one thousand, in competition," an angler replied.

"How's it going? Caught anything?" I asked, scanning his tack. "Don't you get bored?"

"Not, a chance," he said. "Too much banter around here."

"What, the splash of the odd fish and grumble of an angler who'd claim his catch, each one the biggest, of the day?" I jested.

"No, No. You've missed the point," he said, "Fishing is about casting – throwing out your line, then waiting for the catch." I must have looked confused. He explained, "Your mind provides the banter. And waiting creates silence for your answers to land.

"So, you could say, you go fishing to meditate?" I suggested.

"Peace and quiet," he said, winking and doffing his cap.

I crouched down to see their catch — they hadn't managed much. We swapped stories of the ones that got away and I told them how I'd once been the star rooky on an eco-island off the northeast coast of Queensland, Australia. I was the only one to reel a catch and turned proudly to show my instructor

"Don't touch it!" The instructor screamed in panic. "It's deadly." I'd waved a poisonous puffer fish in his face.

We all laughed.

"If you want to try your hand at fly-fishing, Kiwi style, you're in the perfect place," one of the men said. I wanted to tell them it might be the perfect place, but I was far from having the perfect time.

"Tongariro Lodge," one fisherman pointed. "That's where you want to go. Special access to rivers on private land. Heli-fishing, too." They all nodded in unison.

"It's enough to raise the blood pressure of any fisherman worth his salt," said another. "You can catch trophy trout like nowhere else on earth – they say over fifty thousand prime-conditioned wild rainbow and brown trout migrate there seasonally."

I whistled. If only. Thanking them for the tip I trudged back to the hotel – my Taupo catch was more wet fish than trophy trout. It was such a shame. I'd fallen in love WITH Taupo, not IN Taupo.

Back in the room, I was relieved to find Himself asleep on the bed. I gingerly passed to the balcony where I clandestinely nestled to think. What would I do about this predicament I'd gotten myself into? Had it not been for my friend's recommendation, I was certain to have been cagey about Charles's emails and deliberately misleading photograph. I drew a deep breath, let out a big sigh and took stock — I didn't want to create bad blood between us or upset the holidays for him and his guests. Perhaps they'd dilute the situation and be my salvation – I could only hope.

=><=

Charles had selected special activities for each of us. On Christmas Eve, his nephew, Andrew, and I would set sail on the Spirit of New Zealand, a 148ft barquentine square-rigger, a three-mast schooner; it could reach fourteen knots under sail.

I considered Andrew a gift from the gods. His lively,

innocent and chatty nature made him easy to hang out with, and I shamelessly used him to escape Charles's increasingly unwanted attention. Unlike Charles, he was too skinny for his own good. He had an aristocratic air belied by his ghost white skin and unnaturally bleached mop of hair. He was a nice lad with a confident smile that matched his almost translucent grey, friendly eyes.

It was perfect weather for sailing. We walked the plank through a hoard of people along the unsightly commercial docks as a hesitant call was repeated from the crow's nest: "Those not sailing, please leave the ship." The crew politely hurried along those departing, and with the last safely ashore, the gangplank raised – I was delighted to be finally free of Charles. I'd begun vigilantly monitoring where I was in relation to Charles all the time – to avoid him constantly encasing my hand in his large, pappy maulers.

I breathed a sigh of relief as the ship calmly drifted from the dock, leaving him behind.

Once out of the harbour we were offered refreshments from below deck. I was as keen as a kid to explore what lay below. At first I couldn't venture past the serving area, but I managed to convince a crewmember to secretly show Andrew and I around once the queue for cakes and coffee dwindled.

I followed Sonja eagerly as she escorted me through a section of the living quarters; the old bunks, narrow and plentiful, were equally split between male and female, until recently, when expeditions grew more popular with women.

"How many crew are there?" I asked her.

"There's around fifty of us looking after forty youth development trainees," she replied.

"Wow! I feel really lucky to be aboard such a beautifully crafted, majestic vessel," I enthused.

"How great is this?" I nudged Andrew later, up on deck. We

stood, shoulder-to-shoulder, spellbound by the beauty of the crystal clear waters.

"I wish I could go on a longer voyage, like the trainees," he said, with a hint of jealousy.

"Perhaps, you can?" I said, "You're probably too old to be a trainee, but what about some other way?"

"Nah, I doubt they'd be interested in me," he said, defeated.

"Well, you'll never know if you don't ask!" I encouraged, with a forceful nudge. "Go, create the opportunity mate – you've got nothing to lose. And, if you don't get what you want this time there's always another. There are plenty of similar activities out there in the world – go look for them!"

"Is that how you see the world?" he asked. "Must be an exciting way to live."

"Life's full of opportunities of all shapes and sizes!" I agreed. "That is exciting! But the big question is, whether you can recognise them when they present themselves to you."

"Sitting around waiting for something to happen's never really been my style," I went on. "Dreams have no value for me unless I act on them. I need to keep moving, keep doing."

"And how is that working out with Uncle Charles?" Andrew asked, sending me a sly glance.

"Hey. If I hadn't accepted this opportunity from your uncle we wouldn't be having this conversation," I said, hoping he'd get my drift. "And I wouldn't have this sensational, once in a lifetime experience."

"I haven't always thought this way," I went on slowly. "But I always regret the opportunities I miss out on. Once, as a twenty two year old, I was asked to try out for Operation Raleigh – a sustainable volunteer organisation. I wanted to spend six months in Borneo helping at Kalimantan Orangutan Sanctuary. Part of the selection process was trekking in the jungle. I couldn't afford to buy hiking boots so I borrowed some. I ended up with blisters to the bone and had to bow out of the running."

"How did you feel about that?" asked Andrew.

"Pretty pissed at the time," I replied. "I often wonder where life would have delivered me if it had been otherwise."

As I was speaking I suddenly saw a pattern emerging – my Borneo failure was just like my UNESCO fiasco. I'd had a dream, only for it to be dashed by bad luck and ill health. It seemed like – despite all the wonderful things I'd done in my life – the opportunities I'd striven for continued to elude me.

"What's for you won't go by you!" I said to Andrew, hoping it was true. "At least I tried!" Privately I wondered. Would my journey have been different had my luck taken a different path? Or would I have arrived at this destination regardless?

The abundantly reflective shine on magnificent timber decks made them seem plastic coated. The wooden rail that ran around the edge of the deck and the stainless steel fittings gleamed in the sunlight, not a fingerprint to be seen. I imagined the deck hands doing a Mr Miaggi for hours – polish on, polish off, polish on, polish off, like the Karate Kid. Believe me, I understood the efforts of polishing silverware – I thought of my grandfather and how, as a child, I'd polished the family heirlooms – polish on, polish off... I'd started my own collection – age thirteen. My pride and joy was a silver spoon collection dated to the early seventeen century. Although I've been adding new treasures ever since, they've become harder to find.

My mother opened a shop called Cottage Antiques. Imagine a small paned, bow fronted shop window like something from A Christmas Carol. Positioned at the end of a small row of miner's cottages in St. Albans, Hertfordshire, Mum's shop was just like that. One day after school, I waited patiently by the portable Calor gas heater in the small kitchen out back for the little hand to hit 'five'. I was bored. I wanted to go home.

"Home time," I called, just as the shop door opened. My heart sank.

"Not another customer!" I grumped to Mum. It was a

neighbour from a couple of doors along, 'John Spoon' we called him. He kept a small cabinet displaying small antique silver treasures for sale in my mothers' shop. I was often dragooned into polishing his wares, much to my disgust.

"Kim, I have something for you," he called. 'I don't want lollies, I want to go home', I'd thought. He uncurled his hand and my eyes and mouth flew wide open as they could go.

"Is that for me?" I gasped.

"The bowl was damaged, so I made a necklace for you," he said, putting it around my neck.

My pendant had once been a 1714 solid silver teaspoon. John had drilled a hole in the narrow end and put it on a silver link chain. Now, bowless, it hung long, and narrow like a flattened droplet with an upturned end.

"Thank you so much. I'll treasure it – forever," I said.

"No. Thank you," he replied, "You've been so diligent in polishing my silver."

Like all precious things, a frequent spit and polish keeps things at their best. I hadn't been so diligent of late. My spoons had been in storage for a while. Had they lost their sparkle? No more than I have, I thought grimly.

$$=><=$$

Despite my uneasiness with Charles, New Year's Eve 1999 must be one of my most memorable. Celebrations began just after a magnificent seafood lunch in Gisborne. I wanted to stay alert all night, so I chose a satisfying but light meal – crustaceans with a twizzle of fresh spaghettini, gently doused in lemon oil with a side of fresh garden salad and halved cherry tomatoes. Bands played and festivities were well underway by the time we made our way to the beach. Out to sea you could just make out the Spirit of New Zealand as she waited to make her grand entrance.

I was thrilled to see the Maoris preparing for the Haka. Their dramatic outfits and fierce face and body paint always sent a shiver of expectation down my spine. Spectators scurried to claim the perfect spot, pitching themselves on the golden sand to see in a new millennium. We all waited on tenterhooks as performers poised to launch on command. Timing was crucial — everything was to be perfectly synchronised. The Maoris' wakas (canoes) were clearly visible as they escorted the Spirit of New Zealand as she sailed to anchor. The turbulent sea, however, proved too strong: the oarsmen paddled valiantly but most couldn't escape capsizing. From the stage directly behind me, Dame Kiri Te Kanawa welcomed the new dawn with a song, accompanied by the New Zealand Symphony Orchestra. The rendition of Morgan by Strauss included three blasts on a conch as a thousand Maori warriors greeted surviving wakas. The contrast of cultural styles – haka and opera – was simply sensational. The passion emanating from the Maoris as they performed their ancestral war cry was utterly invigorating. I felt the thunder beneath my feet and a reverberation through the air. My emotions were intensely powerful. It felt like something supernatural had taken control of me, the night, the performers – even nature itself. It was special. I felt special.

Our group swiftly moved away from the New Year's celebrations to a cliff top in the middle of nowhere, where Charles had another surprise for us. A Native American Indian shaman from Whitehorse, South Dakota greeted us in front of a large tent. He could have walked straight from a film set – the consummate medicine man. He was simply clad in an oversized, long-sleeved top made of tan coloured suede and loose matching pants. Firmly knotted just above his hips sat a black and red hand-twisted rope. He stood tall, probably a shade over six-foot. His deeply crevassed, mahogany skin was glossy and unblemished, bordered by long, soft, white wavy hair that merged seamlessly with his beard.

I felt like I'd known him all my life.

"My name is Long Leaf," he intoned gravely. "I will lead you into the year 2000. Before you enter the sweat lodge you must strip down to your sarongs and vests. Leave your bags outside and remove your jewellery." He disappeared inside the tent.

I dutifully removed the silver ring with a turquoise stone that came from my aunt's mother-in-law — one of the families last Native American to leave the Indian reservation in the US. It hadn't left my finger since I was thirteen years old. I placed it inside my wallet, leaving it in my bag outside for safekeeping.

Waiting in single file to enter the sacred sweat lodge, I calmed my energy and speculated about the experience to come. Would there be messages or visions from the Spirit world? I recalled the Inuit I'd met in Canada who'd talked of my grandfather and his spirit, how it soared with the eagles. I privately hoped Granddad's spirit would talk to me directly.

Constructed from slender withes of supple saplings bent to form a dome shaped structure, the sweat lodge was lashed together with grass or root cordage and covered with hides to retain its heat and steam. I squeezed awkwardly through the narrow opening. A silent serenity befell the domed space. Feeling instantly drained and disoriented, I panicked. I was suddenly desperate to escape the intense heat emanating from the hot rocks in the middle of the tent. As the shaman sprinkled them with water and sage, the heat intensified. I took my place on the floor directly opposite the shaman. My eyes met his, full of warmth. And it seemed then as if an ancient wisdom had touched my soul. My entire being was pacified – mind, body and soul.

It took a few moments for everyone to get comfortable while, in soft tones, our host explained that sweat lodges were used for purification, prayer, healing or transformation in most modern and ancient cultures. Ritual sweating, with or without ceremonial or mystical significance, had been practiced around the world for centuries. Fifth century BC nomadic Scythians from the Ukraine had used a primitive 'vapour-drug' sweat bath with hempseed thrown on red-hot stones. Then there were the grand bathing facilities of the Roman Empire and Greek baths that inspired the smaller, more modest hammams in Arabic countries. He told us that the early nomadic Finns likely used a portable sweat lodge similar to those carried by the American Indians and tribes of central Asia. Had the Finns introduced the sweat lodge to the American Indians across the Bering Strait when trading fur? Or had it come from the Mayans?

"No one knows," he concluded. "What we do know is this is a place of spiritual refuge and mental and physical healing – a place to get guidance from spiritual entities, totem helpers, the Creator and Mother Earth."

Under my breath, I fervently asked any spirit entities that might be present for an early escape from Charles – a quick jaunt to freedom.

"Here your collective experience has a common purpose," the shaman continued. "To purify your spirit in a place where all sense of race, colour, religion and creed are set aside."

More water was cast over the glowing rocks that nestled in the hollow of the shallow pit, all but a metre away — the air was hot and dry, the heat's intensity spiralling as the ceremony began. We repeated prayers as offerings to the Creator were respectfully thrown into the pit of glowing rocks. Our host gently and rhythmically tapped a drum, a living and breathing entity, calling for protection from the tree and animal spirits from which it was made and that lived within it. As we passed the sacred pipe, drawing on the mixture of tobacco and herbs, the drumbeat silenced and was replaced by an almost inaudible yet seductive chant.

I succumbed to a deep peace, dark and silent far beneath my skin. My physical body felt strong but 'I' was somewhere else – and nowhere, too. A pale man appeared at the edge of my vision – I had the impression it was my grandfather standing tall, with a smile and a look in his eye that said, "You're alright. Just keep going." It disappeared. I screwed my eyes, hoping to get another glimpse. Then a house swam into view – a white, weatherboard with a long Victorian veranda. My mother sat with her legs covered by a rug – a black watch tartan. My brother stood nearby. My sister was delivering tea. I gazed outwards, as if the veranda were a stage, over undulating ground running down to a river snaking down from snow-capped mountains in the distance. I sensed it was my home.

It was the rhythm of the drum that pulled me back to consciousness. Deeply relaxed, I barely felt my body, yet I was unbelievably alert. My mind was empty; I was comfortably oblivious to everything except the chanting that filled the dome. The experience felt deeply familiar, like a primal memory.

"If you feel like singing, please do," uttered the shaman. I was overwhelmed by the urge to add my voice to the others — I suddenly knew the words. How was that possible? Was I talking in tongues? Was it the pipe? Or were the spirits singing through me? It didn't matter. The experience alone was amazing.

I became aware that cold air was beginning to circulate. The exit had been slowly revealed and we filed out as we had entered, in silence. As we emerged, we were greeted by a gloriously uninterrupted view of the new millennium sun rising over the sea. It felt like I'd made a fresh beginning – mind, body and soul.

I'd once made a promise to Dougal. No matter what happened, no matter where I was in the world or what I was doing, on the strike of midnight on December 31st I'd look to the sky and wish him a Happy New Year. I was a little late this year, it was already January 1, but I was sure he'd understand.

"Wherever you are. What ever you're doing - Happy New

Year my love," I whispered under my breath. "May it be your best one yet!"

I went to retrieve my belongings. Grabbing my turquoise ring I was horrified that it had changed from a circle to what looked like half a heart. It was as if it had been re-forged – no amount of pushing or pulling would bring it back to shape. I stared down at what seemed like a message from beyond.

=><=

Despite the sensational, once-in-a-lifetime experience he'd organised, Charles would not prove to be my other half. I devised a tactful exit as soon as possible, saying I wanted to see more of New Zealand, which had begun to look like paradise on earth to me.

Happy to be on the move, again, travelling through its lush forests, sandy beaches, turquoise lagoons and over picture book mountains, I was in seventh heaven and didn't want to leave.

There was a mad moment on the road between Nelson and Picton. I, hurtling along, at speed, throwing the car around every bend like Stirling Moss. The road was clear so I made the most of every bend – a chicane. Oops – reverse. I pulled aside to follow a homemade sign that read: 'Jewellery Maker'. The incline of the unmade road got steeper and steeper as it climbed to a cabin at the top.

Greeted by Alan the resident artist, my first impression was 'this guy needs to eat!' Emaciated and fair-haired, he was nevertheless well groomed and dressed in the ubiquitous knee length shorts and air brushed T-shirt, thongs – flip-flops, for some. As he shook my hand I noticed he had kind eyes and a smile to match.

As I perused a showroom gallery exhibiting works of art usually reserved for London, Paris, Rome and New York, he made me a coffee, I told him about the misshapen ring and how I hoped to find the other half. And told me his story. We retired to the veranda shaded by a corrugated iron roof looking over the lakes and hills below. I sat and listened without a care in the world.

"I was a young man fresh out of a London Art school when I took off to experience Europe and its great historical works then through Indonesia, Australasia and New Zealand. But my journey came to a grinding halt in Germany when I met the love of my life - Helena" he said, with glistening eyes. "Top up?" he asked, as he turned his back.

"I've also travelled half way around the world to find love, so I know exactly what you mean," I said, feeling a connection. "So, how did you end up here?"

"For years, we travelled and worked on a pittance. I never really got into my art until, at an exhibition in South America, Helena and I had an enormous fight," he said, grinning.

"Why the grin?" I enquired.

"It's funny how things work out," he sighed. "I was filled with anger and regret for not having kept to my plan. So, I decided to start where I'd left off all those years ago." Thinking of my own situation, I wondered how many people change their life plans to be with someone, only to not have it work out.

"By the time I reached New Zealand, Helena and I had made up but she wouldn't leave Germany to live here," he gestured to the landscape beyond. "This was my dream home. So we parted ways."

"That's a shame," I said, "But you still seem happy with your dream – even without Helena."

"And what about your story?" asked Alan.

"I've also changed my plans for potential love," I said, laughing and shaking my head. "But fortunately it was only a detour. Things didn't work out." I told him about Charles, how disappointed I'd been not to find love and how desperate I'd been to get away.

"From the minute I set eyes on him I knew we wouldn't work out," I shrugged. He had no self-respect, no compassion. Despite his generosity, I felt he didn't really care about my welfare so long as I fulfilled whatever fantasy he'd had about the two of us. He didn't even seem to notice that we had nothing in common no interests, beliefs, or values. There was no laughter, real conversation or fun, just aggravation and hard work.

"In the end I had to tell him it was clear there was nothing between us, that I should go," I told Alan.

"So. How did Charles take your suggestion?" asked Alan, not wanting to let things go.

"Better than I'd thought," I explained, "In a very calm, expectant manner, Charles simply replied, "Yes. You're probably right."

I'd told him, "I truly appreciate your kindness. I've had such a wonderful time. And, I'll treasure the memories forever. Thank you," I'd said, with sincerity.

But, I hadn't expected his rejoined, "Well. You're not as I'd expected. You've got a solid brick wall around you," he'd said then, a little angrily. "You need to pull it down or you'll get nowhere with any fella."

"I knew he'd said it to hurt me," Alan, "But, I couldn't help wondering if he was right?"

Alan offered me lunch on the veranda but said he had to get back to work. It was just a sandwich, my thoughts, and me. Looking out at the calm, glimmering water through a mystical, magical forest, relaxed in the warmth of the sun, I dreamed of a wood cabin by a hill or lake of my own.

In that brief meeting with Alan, I learned something about connection, about how one thing always leads to another. I'd understood that nothing works in isolation. Every choice or decision creates an action, re-action or non-action that impacts the swing of your pendulum – like a plumbline, we're permanently connected, adjusting our compass. But in the end we're all the same – our momentum swings from one thing to another. If it hadn't been for Charles I wouldn't have travelled across New Zealand, nor met Alan and ... how far should I go? I began to explore the flood of inspiration washing over me. The surrounding landscape was having a profound effect. I thought of Dougal who had recognised years ago that I found peace in nature when he called me 'Kim of the Forest'. I wondered if somewhere in this land of the long white cloud I'd find my place. Could this be the place of peace and stability I sought? Would I belong here?

"I hope you find what you're looking for," called Alan as I waved goodbye to him and the beautiful place he lived that had so captured my heart. Driving back down the mountain, I thought about the fact that I was supposed to head off to Melbourne the next day – but what would happen if I didn't? No one was waiting for me there. I was a free agent. Who was to stop me making New Zealand home?

===><===

9

AUSTRALIA

Buddha once said, "With our thoughts we make our world." That is to say, if you can imagine it, it can be. So, with great excitement, I envisaged a new life in New Zealand. I scoured the want ads and 'homes to let' columns. I dropped by the local government job centre for guidance on where to look. As I walked the city registering with recruitment agencies, I popped my head into every office or building that showed signs of work to be had. It was exhausting. But, just as I decided to call it a day, I spotted another recruiters' hoarding — okay, this would be the last.

As I passed my completed form to the receptionist, I explained that I'd just arrived in Auckland, was staying at the YMCA and looking for somewhere more permanent and a job; any work would do for the time being.

Before heading back to the 'Y', I walked the harbour. I was feeling optimistic, nostalgic and brimming with enthusiasm. I splashed out on swanky meal at one of the trendy bars on the waterfront and gazed at the yachts preparing to race in the America's Cup. As I watched my new world come alive, I imagined a wee house by the beach at Devonport, a gorgeous enclave, and a job in the city so I could take the ferry to work each day.

Ten days later I'd moved from the 'Y' into a home of my own just as I'd imagined it. I called it 'Butlin's Holiday Shack' – a private joke because it was actually a rather large two-story property with views over Devonport's roofs, tropical gardens and banana trees to a quiet, secluded beach. Not quite the lakeside place I'd imagined on the ferry crossing – but I had to start somewhere. My neighbours were gentle, welcoming folk. Even the big ginger Garfield-like cat sat waiting on my doorstep for a treat from me made it feel like home. My new favourite Pohutukaua trees lined the street with their brilliant red flowers showering the pavements below.

I was over the moon when I wangled a four-week temping job with an iconic British company, quickly extended to a twelve-month contract. The niggling weight lifted from my shoulders – I'd make the rent and my plans were secure for at least a year. I was checking all my boxes and at last it felt as if I was ahead in my quest to secure a place to belong and purposeful work. Now I just had to focus on finding my people – but I was sure that would follow. I finally had a spring in my step.

Then, five months after my New Zealand dream had begun in earnest, I was thrown a curve ball that sent me spinning, again. Work asked me to manage the transformation project from its Regional Head Office in – you guessed it – Melbourne.

=><=

Melbourne

I couldn't help but wonder – had fate played her hand? After all, I'd set out from Scotland in pursuit of an alternative life in Australia. But, somewhere along the way, I lost focus. Jumping

in with both feet, I'd grasped every opportunity that had
presented itself as I passed through each place I'd visited and
New Zealand seemed like it was the place I was supposed to be.

But then I'd ended up on Melbourne soil regardless. Had I
simply delayed the inevitable?

Relocating to Melbourne wasn't a decision I'd taken lightly
— to secure permanent resident status in New Zealand I had to
live and work in the country for two consecutive years. Leaving
with less than a year under my belt had meant forfeiting all
chances for permanent residency.

But the prospect in Melbourne was also a good one. I was in
my element. The job was full of complexity, variety and
potential problems for me to resolve – I always loved a
challenge and it was a chance to really make my mark and push
my career forward. Not to mention the added bonus – I'd have
my dearly beloved grandmother on tap. Could I really afford to
pass up the opportunity? I packed up my things and headed over
the Tasman to set up a new life – again.

But within three months I received notice – all contractors
'were out!' Surely not me? I'd just arrived. However, I soon
learned my two-year, company-sponsored visa I'd thought I'd
secured back in New Zealand had been revoked – apparently just
a day before it had been issued Australian immigration had
changed the rules. My transportable visa – wasn't. It never
had been.

Seething, I jostled impatiently from foot to foot, repeatedly
prodding the button to call the lift for the twenty-fourth floor.
My mind was numb. I had no rational thought except that HR
was in for it! They'd misinformed me. I'd given up my New
Zealand residency based upon their advice. And now I was in
no-man's land, falling down a chasm of rage faster than Jack
Rabbit. It was just as well, for everyone's sake, that the lift took
a while.

Without personal experience, I doubt anyone could possibly

know the distress I felt. I'd been uprooted from Devonport – a place I'd truly, deeply, believed was my first real chance at a home in a very long time. I'd felt everything coming together at last and then – poof – gone. Now, with an unsold car in New Zealand and enough belongings to fill a house still on a boat marked 'Port Melbourne, Australia' — I was officially moving faster than my stuff.

There was no other way to explain it. I was cursed. I was homeless, jobless, and country-less with just sixty days to leave. The only question before me now was – what options were left to me?

I couldn't muster the energy to resolve my situation, let alone have a positive thought. For a week I moped around the house, shifting from floor to sofa. I was barely able to speak.

"I can't go back to New Zealand. And I'm not ready to return to Britain," I told myself. I wasn't quite ready to give up on my dream of a more stable life. "Without a dream to pursue, what's a life worth?"

At the back of my brain I heard my mothers' chiding: "I got that money for you. That expensive university and you've done nothing with it! What a waste!"

"Well, you know what?" I told her in my head. "It wasn't my fault – you can't say I didn't try! Anyway, I haven't given up yet – someday you'll see. There'll be a reason I have it."

It was in that moment that I think I decided to stay put – maybe for the first time in my life.

My decision gave me impetus. I got off the floor and back to work. In less than a month I'd pulled a minor miracle by collecting my Australian permanent residency visa. Within two months I'd secured a permanent job at a major bank. In six months I'd bought a cute 'doer upper' by the sea in St Kilda. Thrilled to be back on track again, I set about creating my forever home, knocking down walls, building extensions, remodelling the kitchen and adding new bathrooms. I worked

Australia | 169

my backside off and, for two years, I was happy. Then the GFC happened.

=><=

"No! No! No!" I yelled, "Not again!"
"I can't do this anymore!" I hollered, breaking down in tears. Then I got angry.
"So! You've lost your job again. What's the big deal?" I repeated, trying to convince myself it was just another bump in the road. I was the ultimate come back queen – I'd mastered the art of picking myself up and getting back on track. But this time felt different – the news had landed like a bombshell. I searched for work, drawing on every molecule of experience, resources and contacts, all, to no avail. My confidence slid and I glimpsed fear. My guts cried out: "There's no job for you anytime soon. The world's going into melt down." Conscious bills would keep arriving quickly taking my savings with them, I was lost as to what I should do.

Desperate to clear my head, I'd decided to get away for a few days. I needed some time to think things through. I remembered the place by the river where I'd camped with Dougal all those years ago. It would be the perfect spot to reflect and make plans.

I stopped for lunch overlooking a valley of contrasts: rows upon rows of old vine, rooted like soldiers on parade surrounded by the dark, distant, rolling hills. Their metallic-hued, gnarled stems supported a cavalcade of autumn leaves in the process of changing colour. I heard Master Chen's words again: 'Rooting is everything'. I giggled – if only I could get rooted long enough to look like those old Balinese folk gnarled like ancient vines.

A superb platter of local produce was before me, paired with a classic white I sampled at the cellar door. Immersed in splendour, I was relaxed and without a care, forgetting for the moment I was in limbo, again.

I pitched my tent by the mighty Murray River, releasing my anger on the tent pegs as I hammered them into the sun-cracked banks. Settling by the fire, surrounded by giant eucalypts suffering from twelve years of drought, I basked in the tranquillity … until the cheeky Kookaburras chuckled at dusk. All I had to do on this trip was read, swim, reflect and contemplate!

Alone, I lay stretched like a starfish on my well-used tartan billabong rug gazing skyward, my mind drifting away on a fluffy white cloud.

Without warning, a solitary tear dribbled slowly to my ear. The pain of shunning, bullying and being the outsider I'd endured with each childhood move rose slowly and painfully to the surface of my thoughts, dragging with it a deluge of disconnected emotions from somewhere deep within. Soon I was sobbing so hard it felt like I was drowning in a swamp of feelings accumulated over thirty years. "Why? Why can't I get a foothold?" I cried to the sky. "All I want is a home, to be loved. And a reason to be alive."

For decades, I'd done everything I thought I was supposed to. I was relentless, doing everything possible to belong and make a secure, stable home. I'd mastered the art of fitting in. I'd searched far and wide to discover my ideal supportive environment. I'd even sacrificed friends, family, love and freedom. I'd suppressed my creativity for the sake of landing a career. Now I was at the end of my tether.

"What! The fu..ing hell am I meant to do?" I yelled to the wilderness, "I can't go on like this! Help me! Will somebody bloody-well help me!" I cried. "Please, I need a reason to live."

Right on cue, a single kookaburra chuckled above. And I heard Dougal's words from long ago, like a whisper on the breeze. "You should write," he'd said.

Over the years I'd toyed with jotting my ideas down. If not now, when? I asked myself. I reached for my laptop, but I wasn't prepared for the torrent that flowed from my fingers. It was like the words were streaming unconsciously through them – almost as if I was downloading information from a source other than my own brain.

I was flummoxed. I hadn't a clue it was in me. In the sublime stillness, I began writing about the state of the world and what it might take to fix it. I posited it would only take couple of generations, if only we could change the way young generations think and change our expectations. I typed feverishly until I could type no more. Then, exhausted, I surrendered all thoughts and fell into a deep motionless sleep under the bright moon.

When the raucous squawk of the cockatoos' dawn chorus broke my slumber, I realised what I had to do next.

It was time to discover my purpose.

===><===

10

INDIA

Driven by curiosity and a desire to learn – and still with no work on the horizon – I'd begun slowly building up to a little book about the nature of change. It was cathartic and it pushed me to learn more about the world and my place in it. Through a friend I heard about a conference near Mumbai held by an organisation called 'The Initiatives of Change'. Founded by Frank Buchman, an American living in London in 1938, it was dedicated to 'building trust across the world's divides'. I was intrigued.

Taking a chance on my way to the conference, I stopped in Pondicherry to visit a community based on the spiritual writings of Sri Aurobindo. Begun by a French woman – Mirra Alfassa – in 1926 who was known simply as 'Mother' to the ashram's inhabitants, the community was based on Sri Aurobindo's idea that, instead of taking lifetimes to perfect, spiritual realisation could be achieved in a single life. Aurobindo suggested that the purpose of life is to evolve and that human minds can evolve into super minds – to essentially become fully enlightened like a Buddha or Krishna figure.

I liked this idea greatly. Just as Darwinian evolution posits a physical transcendence over time, why not a mental transcendence? Our purpose in life becomes, therefore, to transform the way we think and feel – and wasn't that exactly what my life's journey had attempted?

I arrived in Pondicherry on the commemoration of Mother's death in 1973. It was my first experience of masses on the move towards one location. It was almost impossible to identify people beneath the waves of moving baggage — bags, blankets, children, animals, and whatever else was required as they flocked from all directions. It felt as though the whole country was on the move.

I began to comprehend something of the magnitude and faith that surrounded the community's love for Mother. Pilgrims lined the streets, queuing for days, hoping to 'walk-by' the flower-laden tomb. Entry to the inner sanctum was granted only to those whose birthdays fell within the commemorative week — like me. 'Mother' had died on my birth date — an auspicious sign.

I was curious to see the inner sanctum. My enquiries were overheard by a handsome, unusually tall, well-built, and impressively groomed Indian gentleman.

"Come with me. I'll get you a ticket," he called out in perfect English. He looked like a Bollywood heartthrob.

The hair stood up on the back of my neck as he told me he was in charge of the print shop. Was he a scalper? Would his ticket be a forgery – and what would the guards of the inner sanctum do to me if it were discovered?

"So, what brings you to Pondi," he asked, after introducing himself as Suresh.

"I'm interested in Aurobindo's philosophies, particularly about education," I explained.

"'Build character in your students so they grow up into straightforward, frank, upright and honourable human beings,'" Suresh quoted Aurobindo solemnly.

"Exactly!" I replied.

Back home, I'd read how the ashram promotes the evolution of an 'integral' education, in which children develop the five essential aspects of personality: the physical, the vital, the mental, the psychic and the spiritual. From kindergarten, the centre progressively engendered awareness of the world through observation, creative expression and exploration, an appreciation of beauty in all its forms and the development of the powers of the mind – comprehension, expression, reasoning, concentration, independent and original thinking, assimilation, selection and judgement.

Rather than seeking to bestow knowledge from on high, the idea was to stimulate students to evoke knowledge from within. Aurobindo believed children were essentially souls with a body, life-energy and mind that needed to be helped to develop integrally and harmoniously. "The new aim is to help the child to develop his or her intellectual, aesthetic, emotional, moral, spiritual being and his communal life and impulses out of his own temperament and being," he wrote. I liked the idea. It suggested that the words I'd begun to write – about the spiritual desert the West had created in its obsessive quest for more – might have something to do with the integral knowledge lying dormant within me. Further, it intimated one of the keys to changing this was through better education and understanding.

"Could you point me in the right direction of the ashram, please?" I asked.

"Yes. You're standing in it. It's right here!" He laughed cheekily.

I was confused. It didn't look much like an ashram to me. I'd expected a rather large compound with dilapidated, washed out yellow or pink buildings, interiors covered in reams of bright red and yellow flowing fabric, embossed with beads and tassels in silver or gold. I'd thought to see gaudy statues of deities surrounded by small mercies left by fervent worshipers. Instead the ashram was more like a town with every kind of store available selling goods made locally by the 'ashramites'. It even had its own steelworks, water purification plant and public transport system. It was quite an amazing place.

"And where's the school?" I asked.

"First, your ticket. Then I can take you to the school," he said.

Exiting the Administration Bureau with a ticket that included lunch, Suresh refused reimbursement. It was humbling to have received something from one who seemingly had so little. I wanted to express my appreciation, so I offered a copy of my writings, which he accepted graciously.

"Are you a teacher?" he asked.

"No. Just curious," I replied. I explained my writing had prompted this trip to explore the world more fully and understand how I could use my unique skills to make it a better place.

"They call it automatic writing," Suresh nodded knowingly when he heard me describe how the torrent of words had flowed from me. "It's as though you're on autopilot if you know what I mean? Like you're not really there when you're writing."

Well, I wasn't so sure about that. I was well and truly present when I felt my fingers 'owned by something else'. I'd been aware of the strange sensation travelling down my arms as my numbed fingers freely keyed the words. It really was quite an extraordinary experience – and no, I hadn't been smoking anything.

"Spiritualists claim the words come from a supernatural source," he continued. "Did you feel as if a spirit took control of your hands to write the words through you?"

"It's an interesting idea," I mused. "But perhaps it was just my subconscious mind?" I wasn't quite ready to accept some other force had been speaking through me, but it was food for thought. Plus, it was the first time I'd spoken of such things out loud and I felt awkward. But when Suresh didn't bat an eyelid, I warmed to the subject. I realised the conversation seemed quite normal to him – after all, I was in India, where spiritual seeking had been second nature for millennia.

After we'd spent a good hour discussing Sri Aurobindo's philosophies over cups of tea I headed back to my hotel room to rest. But my mind was too active to sleep. Like a record on repeat, I kept wondering: Should I go to the tomb? I shouldn't. Go to the tomb, don't go to the tomb – I'd make a decision then change my mind just as quickly. I couldn't find peace. I worried what would happen if I reneged on my commitment to view the tomb with Suresh – how would he feel if I pulled out – especially as he'd so kindly bought me a ticket?

I lay in bed, hands together, fingers pointing north and prayed to Krishna: "Please let Suresh understand!" I sent out thanks for all the help Suresh had given me and everything I'd experienced in Pondicherry, the great kindnesses I'd received from the poorest people, whose extraordinary willingness to share whatever little they had was deeply humbling.

Eventually, I concluded the timing was too tight between my trip to the tomb and my flight to the conference.

"Suresh, I'm really sorry, but I can't meet you tomorrow," I called him on his mobile phone. "I can't take the risk of going to the tomb and missing my flight."

I felt his silence.

"I'm so sorry," I repeated.

"Are you sure?" he asked. No, I wasn't. But it was late and it wasn't fair to convey all my inner turmoil.

"I understand," he said finally and wished me safe travels.

I felt terrible that I'd discarded Suresh and the efforts he'd made in getting me a ticket for the auspicious occasion. Had I thrown away a once in a lifetime opportunity for enlightenment? What inspiration might I have received on such an auspicious occasion? Instead, I'd spend my birthday travelling. 'What's for you, won't go by you' passed through my thoughts and with that, I finally fell asleep.

As it happened, the driver was late. Then we stopped for the morning newspaper, a garland of flowers and finally left the flowers with a roadside idol in exchange for protection and safe passage before we were on our way. By that time, it was me he needed protection from.

As we neared ancient sandstones I'd seen the previous day, I laughed disbelievingly as he repeatedly insisted we stop. It was as if the powers that be wanted me to stay in Pondicherry. Was it a message that I should slow down, stop moving so quickly from place to place and develop the inner knowledge to determine which opportunities are worthwhile, rather than grab at everything that comes my way? I sat in deep contemplation for the rest of the journey.

Thankfully the pilots were also on Indian time, and I made my flight with plenty of time to spare. I thought about the angst I'd put myself through getting to the airport – and, for the first time, realised how much of it was so unnecessary. My driver hadn't tried to slow me down, he was teaching me a lesson in patience. I'd been the hare and he'd been the tortoise – he was showing me that slow and steady wins the race.

The driver also made me realise that in rushing off from the ashram I'd passed up on a once in a lifetime opportunity – just so I could pursue the possibility of another opportunity that wasn't even fully realised. I determined then that – for Suresh's sake – I'd make the most of any chance that presented itself to me for the rest of the trip.

=><=

precursor to Hinduism – the language of its holy book, Avesta, was closely related to Vedic Sanskrit. I was fascinated by the religion and wanted to learn more.

"Our standing in India is rather peculiar," Mr Rao explained enthusiastically. "We're Indian nationals, yes, but our cultural and religious practices are not."

"What does your religion tell you?" I enquired.

"Actually, we're generally not concerned with theology – our religion is our identity not some formal teaching," he said.

A light went on in my head. I'd gone in search of my culture, not realising that it was already a part of me, ingrained in my very being. Whether I liked it or not, I was British born and bred. Part of the problem was that the customs and traditions of my homeland were an anathema to me. I'd never understood them, never seen their value or their purpose. But listening to Mr Rao it dawned on me that I had no real identity – I didn't know who I was and therefore I belonged everywhere and nowhere.

When I finally tuned back into our conversation, Mr Rao was describing the Parsi initiation ritual and I couldn't shake the feeling that it strangely paralleled my own life.

"It begins with a ritual bath then a spiritual cleansing prayer; the child changes into white pyjama pants, a shawl and a small cap," he was saying. Following introductory prayers, the child was given sacred items associated with Zoroastrianism – a shirt and cord, *sudre* and *kusti* – then faces the main priest. Fire was brought in to represent God. Once the priest finished the prayers, the child was formally part of the community and religion.

I reflected my own initiation into teenage-hood had similarly been marked by fire. Unlike the other catholic kids I schooled with, I didn't take first communion. Instead, for my thirteenth birthday I got to choose which restaurant my parents and I would go to – just them and I, no siblings allowed. Unfortunately, my night out was delayed by my contracting scarlet fever – the first

I set out on the long journey from Mumbai to a hill station renamed the Centre of Governance, high upon the Asian Plateau where the Corporate Sustainability Conference I was attending would be held over seven days. The freeway ended abruptly on a dirt track, upon which we bounced from one pothole to another. Relief came when the consistently dull grey scrub was replaced by lush vegetation as we entered Panchgani village and its relatively smooth surfaced road. As the driver made a tight right-hander into the station, scraping the ornately carved sandstone arch we turned into an extensive garden filled with intensely coloured exotic plants. I felt a jolt of recognition as a magnificent eagle entered into frame — it was a good sign that my personal mascot was there to greet me. It made me feel as if I might finally be on the right track to discovering my purpose.

Among many crises engulfing the world, one of the most palpable is governance — it affects millions. Nestled on a sixty-eight acre campus overlooking the Krishna Valley, the Centre for Governance's mission is to strengthen such capacity across government, non-profit and public sector organisations. Over the following week I would attend lectures, seminars, workshops and round tables hosted by policy-makers, thinkers and practitioners debating a range of far reaching topics.

I particularly enjoyed the factory visit. Although the relatively large, privately owned factory was immaculate, it was the owner – Mr Rao – that impressed me most. I was curious about his unblemished, porcelain white skin – I'd thought it strange for an Indian and asked after his heritage.

"My people were descended from Persians who came here many centuries ago to escape Zoroastrian persecution," Mr Rao proudly told me of his Parsee (Parsi) origins.

I knew a little about Zoroaster. He'd taught that it was each individual's duty to make a choice between good and evil. There was some debate whether the Zoroastrian religion was the instance of fire. Then the dress my grandmother made me for the occasion – an old fashioned blue and mauve thing I hated – caught fire while I warmed myself by the fire waiting for my parents to drive me to the restaurant. I'd come to think this comedy of errors had marred my rite of passage into adulthood. Now hearing Mr Rao's explanation I suddenly wondered if by accident I'd been initiated as Zoroastrian!

Interestingly, I saw some parallels between Zoroastrian and Sri Aurobindo's thought, mostly in the idea that we're self-creating – that it is the dynamism between good and bad that forges the self. Since I'd left Scotland, I'd been running from one place to another, feverishly trying to find my place, flitting between meaningful work and pointless corporate work, meeting good people and bad, looking for my grand purpose in every corner of the planet. I'd wanted only the positive experience, not realising that everything is a combination of both. But I was learning. As long as I remained open, I knew my purpose would become clear.

= > < =

"Hello. You must be Kim?" The portly, bearded, grey-haired gentlemen presented his hand. "I'm Herr Helmut, the Conference Manager. I do my best to help delegates achieve their goals here."

"Yes," I said, drawing a small wicker chair closer. I gave him a synopsis of my writing and my time in Pondicherry. He begged me to call him 'Fred'.

"So, what are you seeking here? " he asked encouragingly.

"I'm seeking three things – purpose, place and people. I regularly secure one or two, but never all at once," I explained. "I'm focusing on my purpose right now – I've long felt I have a job to do, one that will make a difference for the greater good."

"And what do you imagine this purpose might be?" He asked, without giving me a chance to think. "What does it *feel* like?"

"It's like championing justice," I struggled for words, taken aback by the question. "Or helping future generations somehow."

"Well, my dear. You've certainly come to the right place," Fred said. "Let's see what we can muster."

I'd never been somewhere where every person you met seemed eager and willing to help you fulfil your dreams. Over the course of the conference it seemed every conversation yielded an opportunity of interest. I found valid reasons for wanting to accept them all, but my promise to Suresh in the back of that cab outside Pondicherry kept me from taking off in every direction at once. It was more important to give sufficient time to each opportunity, to fully understand the gifts or guidance I was being given.

The first I accepted was an invitation to give a speech to a MBA class at the International University in Pune on how to balance a successful business career with family responsibilities and expectations. I'd expected twenty students or so – something low-key, informal and personal. But when I arrived I found two hundred people poised waiting for me. I hadn't really prepared much – what the heck I would say to them?

My first ever public speaking engagement turned out to be very exciting. I talked about my corporate roles – the projects, the often long, unpredictable hours, how it was difficult to commit to anything requiring regular attendance or time. Most of the students were concerned about how they would balance family life with a western-style corporate career. I explained about mastering the art of juggling.

Ultimately I surprised myself. I walked the stage, relaxed and in control, fielding questions for longer than scheduled.

Speaking in public felt so natural to me. I'd felt a surge of inner power as my voice soared. On that stage I was incredibly alive. I wanted to punch the air and yell, "Yes! The eagle has landed! And one of her purposes is to speak publicly!"

Another opportunity presented itself when I joined a small group of six people clambering up a steep bank in the middle of the night to watch the sun rise over a valley. We celebrated the breathtaking sangria morning with gulps of cooled water from plastic bottles, practised yoga, or sat alone in meditation. As I gazed skyward, my eyes caught sight of ravens and kites soaring high above the towers beyond the valley.

It was there I met Priya. Born of Malaysian Indian-Sri Lankan heritage, she was taller than the Indians around us, her eyes dark and expressive, her hair a long, wiry black mane.

I told her of my experiences in India so far, about the factory tour and my conversation with Mr Rao and what I learned at Pondicherry. I also told her I'd just received an invitation from Mr Gupta – a semi-retired Minister from Delhi who I'd seen speak the day before.

Proud of some of his achievements, he mostly expressed regret for being less than adequate in improving the lives of the region's youth while in office. I listened intently, taken in by his gentle, wise tone. I'd felt quite sad for him – he appeared to be a good, well-intentioned gent.

"Around a hundred of my semi-retired colleagues had fought for social change, during our time in office. We each felt we could have done more in our official capacities, so we've committed to continue our cause in fighting for social change," he'd explained to me when I approached him after his talk. "We meet once a month, in Delhi. I'd be honoured if you would attend and bring your skills with you. Perhaps you could be of service?"

It all sounded very interesting. And, I must admit, I was very keen to attend, even if only to find inspiration. In fact, I was leaning towards heading to Delhi next – I'd promised Suresh I'd see any exciting new opportunities through to their conclusion and I was going to be true to my word.

"And what of you?" I asked Priya.

"I first trained as a speech therapist. But then I pursued pattern therapy before developing a programme for children with learning disabilities that I run at my school in Malaysia," she said. "I'm in India to see if I can entice Sadhana in Mumbai to adopt my program."

"What is pattern therapy?" I asked, intrigued.

"It's been around in its current form since 1955, when a neurologist called Fay Temple picked up on a largely discredited theory," she explained. "I don't know how much you know about the evolution of an infant brain. But, perhaps you know it evolves chronologically, through stages of development similar to first a fish, a reptile, a mammal and finally a human?"

"No. My knowledge is pretty scant," I replied, thinking I knew a bit about neurology as a result of researching MS but that was about it. "I do understand brain growth and development are a dynamic, always changing process."

"When a child can't see, hear or feel properly, they can't respond to the world in the right way," Priya continued. "For instance, severely damaged brains may have serious sensory learning and motor problems. Moderately damaged ones might be significantly challenged in one or all of these realms and mildly injured children may have learning, behaviour, coordination or speech problems for their age level."

Captivated, my thoughts jumped into business mode. Connecting my thoughts, writing and what I learned in Pondicherry, I wondered whether here was an opportunity to get closer to my purpose. I quizzed her on her programme, keen to know more.

"It's designed to treat the brain — the root cause, not the

symptoms," she explained enthusiastically, warming to her subject. "We speed up the natural process with visual, auditory, and tactile stimulation, and increase the frequency, intensity, and duration of these stimulations to match the way a human brain grows in an orderly fashion."

"I guess you work on the premise of the old adage, 'use it or lose it!' I joked.

"Indeed," she replied, "For more than half a century similar programs have run on the fact that the brain grows by use."

"It's a pretty good selling point for 3A universities, too," I added. "Can your work help older generations too?"

As Priya told me how she'd helped her eighty-something-year-old father recover his eyesight with some simple exercises, I wondered if there was something magical in her toolkit for my shitty leg, too. I'd been chuffed as punch with its recovery since the last serious attack in Spain, but I was conscious it still wasn't one hundred percent.

We spoke at length about whether education could set the world on a new, more hopeful and inclusive trajectory.

"So, what are your interests Kim? What are you really looking for?" she asked.

I told her briefly about the UNESCO sponsored program and my failed search for an alternative, meaningful life.

"I feel like a puffer fish snared by the corporate sector that cast me back out to sea without a care because I'm not quite right." I surprised myself that I could laugh as I said it – I *was* healing.

"Would you be interested in joining me on the project?" She suddenly asked, skewering me with those intense eyes.

Was this the door I'd hoped would open? Was this an inkling of a meaningful purpose? I asked the Earth's Keepers for help. I was captivated by her vision, but still wasn't sure if Mr Gupta's offer was a better route to my purpose.

"Please," I begged. "Give me a sign. If Priya makes me an offer, should I take it?"

"I'd love to try if you'll have me," I blurted without another thought.

She beamed. I beamed. It was a beam-fest. And I knew I was on my way.

=><=

Mumbai

I'd arrived late. For the first night, I'd booked a lovely clean room at the YMCA with an en-suite shower on the ground floor, just along from reception. I took a brief wander before hitting the hay under a crispy white bed sheet.

In the early hours I was woken by a scratching sound. I lay deathly still. Where was it coming from? Was it a mouse? A rat? Paralysed for what seemed an eternity, eyes wide in the dark, I finally figured out it was in my bag. There was nothing edible in there, so perhaps the vermin would wander off elsewhere. Slowly, I reached for the lamp switch. Zap and scurry, the long tail disappeared under the door.

"Well, that's the end of sleep for me," I shivered. Instead I lay, a contented smile on my face, thinking about Panchgani and the people I'd met. It had been my first experience of a real gathering of community-minded people and I was hooked on the emotion it engendered. From the moment I'd arrived I'd felt part of the team, even though, technically, I was a one-time visitor. I basked in the glow of feeling part of a community at last.

It wasn't long before the night spooks got a hold of my thoughts though. The inevitable questions brought with them doubts that tossed around and around my head keeping me wide awake. Had I chosen the right opportunity? What use would I be to Priya? I had no hands-on experience working with kids, let alone disabled children. I was sure to let her down and make a fool of myself. Perhaps I should have gone to Delhi? At least I'd well-honed skills to offer Mr Gupta. I thought about Suresh and wondered, would he have approved of my choice and the way I'd made it? Had I taken sufficient time in choosing? I was taking a chance, but what if I'd got it wrong?

"Right, or wrong, it's too late," I told myself, finally. "You made the call. Now just get on with it and do your best. What will be will be."

The next morning – bleary eyed – I relocated to a brand new suite next to Priya at Sadhana. We were relatively secluded behind the patrolled gates of the well-maintained campus – the beautiful space in the middle of Mumbai was a real treat. Eager to explore, I wandered through its intricately carved sandstone buildings and tranquil gardens filled with exotic flowers – it became a kind of sanctuary for me over the weeks to follow.

Despite my worrying, once I understood what to do, I was totally at ease helping Priya run practical activities for the teachers and selected students. Sessions with the children – most of whom had varying degrees of Cerebral Palsy or Down Syndrome – were hilarious. Their antics while vying for our attention were, you could say, creative. We had them creeping, crawling, rolling head over heels back and forth across the mats from one side of the gym to the other. It felt as if we spent more time trying to stop their capers, the children were so happy. It was exhausting but incredibly rewarding.

While Priya undertook other activities – receptive stimulation, expressive activities, masking, brachiation, gravity and anti-gravity exercises and other therapies such as eye patching, amblyopia, flashing lights, auditory stimulation, and identification by touch, I got on with my work

I met with the school's governors and financiers, gathering the information I needed to develop a compelling proposition to entice them to adopt Priya's programme. Most evenings after a stroll around the campus I took to a wrought iron bench, nestled under the most stunning golden flame tree. It was most refreshing, despite of the Mumbai air. The gentle breeze calmed my senses as I pondered the days' activities and sought new inspiration for work yet to be done.

"Priya," I called. "I met a young girl with vacant eyes and a deadpan face who stumbled from one awkward step to the next. She was about five years old. She'd fallen from a high-rise balcony and was physically and mentally damaged – can we help her?"

Watching the young girl, supported on either side by her parents as Priya examined her, I couldn't help but feel a deep inner yearning for her. Her faltering steps, so like my own during an MS attack, reminded me of the little girl I once was – a little girl who'd been so wounded she'd inwardly locked herself away from the world for protection, despite the face she presented to others. She'd lost herself in fear of rejection, disappointment and the inability to find herself an acceptable place in the world. She was driven by the need to feel important, to matter to someone other than herself. In that moment, I realised I hadn't been running away, as my mother had so often berated me. I'd been running to … to something I was yet to discover.

I thought about my MS. Had a fear of losing my legs kept me on the move all these years? Or were they literally trying to tell me to stop running? Had the dream I'd falsely interpreted as my mother perched on my veranda under a black watch tartan rug instead of me prevented me from finding my purpose all this time? I recalled the promise I'd negotiated in Spain for a nugget of gold: "Give me more time and I'll do my job, but not without my legs." Then I wondered what would become of me should MS come to collect. With tears in my eyes I asked who would be there for me – to hold me up? I had nobody. It wasn't a happy realisation.

I found it hard to refocus on the little girl in front of me – it was as if I had suddenly become lifeless. Pressed for time, I knew there was little opportunity for Priya and I to work the child's fragile body, so despite my sudden lethargy I followed Priya's instructions to the letter. We lay her on her stomach and moved her limbs. Our job was much easier once she stopped resisting and we began to see small signs of improvement soon after. The following evening, we made a ramp from floor to bed with an old sheet of ply and taught her parents a new set of moves — creeping motions. The girl resisted again, but once she settled, we began to see more small results. They weren't life changing but expression grew on her face and there was new life in her eyes — a glimmer of hope.

Finally, the hours I'd spent investigating, discussing, calculating and drawing up legal documents culminated in a proposal submitted to the School's principal, who would in due course present it to the Board of Governors. We'd organised presentations and demonstrations, invited parents, teachers and possible investors who would support the adoption of this groundbreaking program despite its challenge to cultural attitudes.

We crossed our fingers that investors would be secured — but only time would tell.

=><=

Sri Lanka

Priya flew to Sri Lanka to have Christmas with her family so I played tourist while waiting for my return flight home to Melbourne.

Unlike the Australian dry heat, Mumbai was very steamy — and that combined with the throngs of people made sightseeing a chore rather than a delight. I had no desire to rush, see and do everything a tourist 'should'. Without a plan I wandered at leisure, absorbed in experiences of my new environment — and kept a vigilant eye on my personal belongings. Mumbai is a metropolis of extremes that must be admired, even if it's not to your personal taste. Everything and anything goes — top-end, glittering high rises stand cheek to jowl with the squalor of slums and the invisible homeless sleeping on the street. Despite the phenomenal inequality, I admired how the city appeared to work. I watched those going about their business both amused and impressed. I laughed and cried in disbelief. It was just like the crazy pictures that frequently circulate the internet — the frail old man with a cow draped over his shoulders, families of six or more on a single pushbike and so on. They work so hard and make less than a basic living wage — there's no welfare cheque in India.

Content just wandering, I found myself near the port by the Gateway to India, which is similar to the Arc de Triomphe but not quite as impressive. I escaped the madness by ducking into the Taj Mahal Palace, a sumptuous five-star hotel that had reopened following a bomb attack in 2000. It must have been my day — a vacant window seat was free, overlooking the harbour and waiting for me.

Through the small panes, I watched the amazing tiffin men, known locally as the 'dabbawalas' who, for millions of people, collect and deliver personal 'dabbas' (lunch tins) every day. Picture this — you leave home for work and sometime during the morning a man on a bicycle collects your hot lunch from your house, then cycles to a central sorting point where your dabba is redistributed for transit by train. Upon arrival at the station, another bicycled dabbawala collects and delivers your dabba to your place of work — hot and in time for lunch — all with a smile and a wiggling head. "Now, that takes some management," I thought. It was synchronicity at its best – but when I realised I was getting excited just thinking how great it would be to have such a complex operation to manage, it became clear I was lacking a career challenge!

Watching the dabbawalas brought my Netherlands friend, Rashi, to mind. I remembered that it was after tasting her cooking that I first promised to visit India. I felt a little sad – dining alone in such a historic venue made me realise how important my friends and family were. They had provided me with the experiences, companionship, laughter and tears I most treasured in life. Rashi had almost been a surrogate mother, not that she was really old enough to be one. But she'd shared her culinary skills, something I really lacked. She'd helped create a community in our wee Hispanic-Dutch house and I missed that sense of connection. Suddenly I wondered what my family would be doing for Christmas – same old, same old no doubt.

There I was, sitting in a lavish, spacious hotel, cool and serene with fresh fish for lunch, in one of the most populous cities of the world — and I realised I might just be yearning for some of that same old. I'd promised myself years ago – on my first independent trip – I'd take advantage of everything I could make life offer. I raised my glass.

"Cheers to a bloody good job!" I said then paused to wonder how good a job I'd really done. At that very moment, my phone rang.

"Hey, Priya, how are you?" I asked, "Good to be home?" I croaked the word 'home' feeling a bit bereft for myself, but great joy for her. She'd been so excited, looking forward to see her parents, especially her father – it had been a while and he hadn't kept too well.

"Hey! You won't believe it!" She exclaimed. "I just received a call from potential investors here in Sri Lanka. They want to meet!"

"That's brilliant! I'm so happy for you. An early Christmas present!" I squealed, overjoyed our hard work had borne fruit. "When will you meet?"

"I told them you're still in India but I'd see if, time permitting, you could join us," she said. "Can you re-schedule your flight? It's on your way home."

"I'll see what I can do," I replied already recalculating flight times in my head. "Let me get back to you when I've got it sorted."

"Great! Oh, by the way – I'm so sorry, but I forgot to thank you for all your hard work at Sadhana. I truly appreciate it. You have such passion for your work. And, you're a natural with the kids," she said as she signed off.

"Oh, I'm not sure about that," I scoffed inwardly, secretly thinking that I was able and enjoyed working for the children but I had discovered I wasn't really the 'hands on' type. Instead I realised I had an amazing breadth of business skills but had never really appreciated how they could be put to use for the greater good.

The realisation had made me feel a little foolish, too. Despite my perpetual motion across the continents looking for meaningful work, I had, in fact, mastered my trade all along. Now I just needed to use it for the right reasons. And I hoped desperately the right door would open soon.

=><=

In the early hours I was woken by the ping of my email — damn, I'd forgotten to turn my phone off. I tried going back to sleep but curiosity got the better of me.

"I don't know if you've heard, but your Grandmother passed away in her sleep last night," it read.

The last time I'd seen my Nan, I'd been anxious. Despite the fact I had a long list of chores and a short time to complete them, I didn't want her feeling rushed. I drew a deep breath to calm myself before entering her room with a flat white in hand; on cold days I took a 'flat white' and on hot, a dark chocolate

'Magnum' ice cream. I was surprised at how 'tuned-in' she was.

"When are you going back?" She'd asked when I'd shown her photos from my first trip to India.

"I'm flying out tonight, Nan," I reminded her.

Looking straight into my eyes, she leaned towards me, rubbed my leg, as she often did, and whispered, "I'd better not keep you then." I felt so bad leaving, but I had to take the opportunity she'd given. I felt she'd known something I hadn't. If only I'd realised that would be the last time I saw her.

At the tender age of ninety-two, she'd had a good innings. I'd always felt so lucky for the wonderful relationships I had with my grandparents — and particularly my grandmother. During my juvenile years I often helped (or hindered) my grandmother as she ran the W.R.V.S. (Woman's Royal Voluntary Service) shop and canteen in one of the local mental hospitals. For twenty years I wrote her what she called 'an epistle' regularly, updating her of my latest news.

For twelve of my adult years we had great times together in Australia — regular picnics and BBQs featuring all her favourite foods including a bottle of red that we would enthusiastically devour, with Granddad in mind, somewhere scenic, usually by a reservoir or spot amongst aromatic gums in the Dandenong Ranges with the kookaburras, rosellas, cockatoos and bell birds. I listened to her stories of the old days and together we put the world to rights. A keen tennis fan, she regularly attended Wimbledon but now Christmas and the Australian Open went hand in hand — making an easy present for me each year — two tickets to the Men's finals.

In latter years she'd struggled to go the distance despite a parking space beneath the stadium. Instead I bought her tickets for the Kooyong Classic with lunch in the members, which we'd enjoy together.

'She never failed to be good company', I thought with pride.

Interesting and interested — that's how I remember her. I hoped people would remember me that way, too.

She'd always end our conversations with a question: "Where are you going?" or "What are you going to do?"

"Oh, I don't know Nan, but I will," I'd always said.

Mentally I saw my grandparents surrounded by majestic gums proudly walking hand in hand into the distance.

I'd miss them for the rest of my life.

===><===

11
THAILAND

I touched down in Suvarnabhumi, Bangkok International, took a domestic flight to Koh Samui, continued to an island somewhere off the South East coast. I then grabbed a shuttle to Big Buddha where I watched malnourished wild dogs wander and fight in the sweltering heat while I waited for the next boat to Koh Phangang — to meet with my Dad for the first time in over 20 years.

Although the long haul had felt like an eternity, I hadn't been fretting over how things might turn out. My inner voice told me everything would be just fine. Maybe it was the scenery – I was thoroughly enjoying my first visit to a Thai island. Relaxed, admiring the scenery and soaking up the sun, I could finally feel a smile cracking on my face — it seemed a long way from India and the thoughts that had dogged me there.

As the boat turned bow and pulled alongside the pier, I craned my neck to see over the heads of jostling passengers hoping to get an early glimpse of my Dad. I didn't know what he would look like — would he be a bit thinner, fatter, shorter, or have less hair? Or would he be fundamentally the same? I made my way along the pier, looking back and forth between the decaying boards and the encroaching crowd expecting our eyes to meet. My awareness sharpened and my heart thundered, until the little voice inside my head reminded me, "It's your Dad you're meeting, silly. He won't be waiting – no one could change that much."

The bay frontage was very small – one bar, one café, a couple of offices and a car park. I checked the bar; his early arrival would likely mean waiting in the background with a cool beer. I so wanted him to come looking for me – just for once. Was I setting myself up for heartache?

I suddenly spotted a four-by-four pull up in the parking lot with the name of my cousin's backpacker resort – Shiralea – scrawled on the side. My initial disappointment was replaced by a creeping hope. The man who jumped out was barefoot, wearing shorts and a t-shirt, his eyes pale blue and crystal clear just as I remembered them. I got a flash of a smile that was similar to mine and a shock of greying hair then — oh boy! — one heck of a hug!

Everything immediately felt so natural, like the last thirty years hadn't happened at all. We simply just picked up where we'd left off. In a way the whole reunion was rather disappointing – not what I'd expected in the least. No overwhelming feelings of elation. No torrents of tears. It was just as though I'd seen him the day before. It wasn't until the resort manager told me my Dad had been so excited that I'd felt a connection. "When you arrived, you should have seen the look on his face!" He'd said. Of course, Dad would never have told me himself – he just wasn't wired that way.

"So, what brings you to my neck of the woods? He simply asked, curious, or perhaps suspicious. "Why now?"

It was kismet really. After the death of my grandmother, I'd come to realise that family was far more important to me than I'd ever considered. I'd called Mum to let her know I'd be heading to my sister's for the family Christmas. It would be the first year in decades I'd done so.

"Did you know your Dad's in Thailand?" She blurted before the words were even out of my mouth.

I'd been stunned. I'd had no communication with him for almost three decades. I'd tried to catch up with him for years but it never seemed to pan out. It's not that we'd argued, and there was no bad blood between us — he just wasn't there. To be honest, I hadn't really noticed his not being on tap – it seemed a normal state of affairs when I was young.

"Mum told me she'd heard on the grapevine that you're in Thailand," I explained to him. "I was in India so I thought I'd drop by."

"You make it sound as if you've popped next door for a coffee and a chat," he laughed.

"Not coffee," I said, "Beer. Come on – It's beer o'clock."

Side by side, we wandered to the bar, settled down on a stool and ordered a drink. I can't say I'd missed him throughout the years — well, not consciously. He was kind of like a fictional character in my life, a story I'd told myself once that had faded over time. I'd hardly seen him since the divorce. As a young adult, I'd be on tenterhooks wondering if he'd come visit me. Because sometimes he didn't even when he'd said he would, and never on birthdays. My family never really celebrated them but I never failed to send Dad a card on *his* birthday. I guess what I was really saying was, "I'm thinking of you. Please get in touch. I miss you and I want you in my life."

He never acknowledged them.

"Hey, remember Switzerland?" I asked, feeling a familiar childish excitement at the memory.

Most of my memories of Dad were to do with travel. He'd sometimes take short haul trips where one of us could accompany him. We each looked forward to our turn – it was such fun exploring new territory with my Dad, not having to share him with my siblings. Years later, I learned my mother had insisted he take one of us with him – he hadn't been keen. I was well into adulthood before I suspected he hadn't ever wanted the responsibility of children. He'd have preferred his freedom to roam, to do things his way, uncompromised. I'd inherited a bit of that independent wanderlust from him, I guess.

One day, when I was ten, the headmistress called me out of class — I'd thought I was in trouble, but didn't know what for. She escorted me to the foyer where my mother was waiting with a small suitcase in hand.

"Where would you most like to go?" Mum asked.

I had wanted to go to Switzerland ever since my Dad had given me a glass pendant containing a dried, pressed Edelweiss flower. So, without hesitation, that's what I said.

"Come on then. Let's go. Your Dad's waiting," she replied.

"Of course I remember," Dad was saying, bringing my attention back to the bar. "How could I forget? You couldn't stop fidgeting in the seat. You were bouncing like a fair ground ride, cackling all the way to the docks at Dover."

We'd driven onto the late boat for the short crossing to Calais. Large commercial vehicles like my Dad's were loaded first. Once they alighted, each driver made a mad dash up metal stairs to the watering hole to drink the crossing away. Dad and I joined them.

"I remember being grateful that you taught me not to be sick despite the Channel's ferocious swell," I said. "I think you were worried you'd have a grumbling kid in the cab."

In fact, the whole journey I'd pretended I was 'Queen of the Road', proudly perched high above the customs officials as they waved us through. Dad popped a couple of Pro Plus pills from the small orange tube he kept hidden in a secret cubbyhole and Tammy Wynett, Johnny Cash, Charles Aznavour and Nana Mouskouri kept us company all night long. I dozed off in the top bunk to the sound of the engine rolling across the continent.

"I'll never forget that morning. At first light, you slammed the cabin door after you'd been at the diner all night. The crushing thud startled me out of sleep," I continued. "I couldn't believe you'd left me there all night – alone."

"Why not?" He chided. "You were fast asleep and safe enough!"

We'd stopped at a truck stop to get a hot dog, the roll warmed by the large metal rod, heated and stuffed through the middle — crispy on the inside, barely warm on the outside, stuffed with a very tasty Bratwurst, almost caramelised fried onions and overzealously squeezed French mustard from the tube. It was standard road fare for truck drivers in those days. And I remembered sheepishly averted my eyes from the concoction, nervous for my Dad to see my hilarity.

"I couldn't believe my sweet, innocent little girl's antics," he laughed when I reminded him.

"You were bored stiff, waiting at the shiny, red, Formica-topped table by the window," he went on. I thought back, remembering how the view was obscured by steam and condensation while I fiddled incessantly with the red and white chequered paper napkins and the 1960s squishy plastic tomato-shaped sauce-pot.

"Remember how you'd squeeze that sauce tomato with such zeal that it would squirt its sticky contents across the table and hit the waitress?" He asked. "That waitress behind the counter always glared at me whenever I came in from that day forward."

"And you said, 'you'd better eat that!'" I retorted. "You gave me a shoulder shrug and a silly grin – not much of an attempt to disapprove of my antics!"

I've always thought my mum was the purveyor of good manners but now I think my father actually contributed more significantly. For instance, at the wimpy on Chequer Street, my brothers and I would noisily suck on the straw to extract the last drop of milkshake from the bottom of a knickerbocker glory glass – to my Dad's chagrin.

"Like a bunch of urchins," he'd said.

"What about the day you saw writing on my palm?" I asked. "I'll never forget what you growled that day – 'You're not some backstreet school kid who can't afford paper!'" I was mortified – not by his words but because I felt I'd let him down. I'd never written on my hand again.

"I remember it was a cold trip," Dad said, returning to the topic of our Switzerland soujourn. "I kept you warm by sitting you on the engine between the two seats as we travelled up and over the snow covered mountains towards Zurich. If I recall correctly, the weather was particularly bad so we didn't get unloaded in time." Trucks weren't allowed on the roads between midnight Friday and midnight Sunday, so we'd been 'weekended'.

"I convinced myself you'd fixed things so you could show me around the city," I told him. First, we'd planned to see the recently released James Bond movie, *Live and Let Die*. Unfortunately, Swiss ratings meant they wouldn't let me in.

"So, after dinner, you had the joy of sitting through …"

"Huh, huh, huh," he grimaced. "Yes, yes. I remember those 101 bloody Dalmatians, with subtitles." He went quiet. I'd made him feel uncomfortable revisiting old times. I cleared my throat and turned to the barman.

"Two more beers, please," I called to ease the tension. After they were placed in front of us I moved the conversation on.

"Anyway. I was in the area so I thought I'd pop by – there's no ulterior motive," I assured him.

"Okay," he rallied. "So what were you doing in India?"

"It's a long story — but I'll tell you anyway," I replied.

"We've got time," he shrugged and flashed that silly grin of his.

$$=><=$$

Over the next few hours, I gave my Dad a potted history of

my travels and how I'd concluded that I needed to find my purpose. I didn't tell him about my MS. I didn't feel he needed to know.

"I've had enough instability, corporate attitudes and turbulence to last a lifetime," I sighed. "This last debacle was the final straw – I'd finally made a home for myself in Melbourne thinking I was done and dusted, contracted as I was to a major Australian bank."

"I was invited to manage a huge, exciting project as a permanent employee," I clarified. "I was so excited. I'd thought my time to settle down had finally come."

"What happened?" He asked.

"I lost my job — and before you ask – it was the GFC to blame this time," I told him.

I explained how I'd travelled half way around the world in search of a dream – Scotland to Holland, then on to Canada looking for a place to really call home and a purposeful, meaningful work.

"I took a chance on love in New Zealand," I explained. "And, when things didn't work out there, I'd opted for a life in Australia."

"From what you've said, perhaps you should have stayed in New Zealand. It sounds idyllic — especially for you?" He said. "You always did love the great outdoors."

"Surely you've gathered by now that my life's never that simple," I laughed, taking another sip of beer. Then I nodded.

"You know I think I could have stayed there forever. But I had places to go, a career to pursue," I mused. I was really touting for feedback. I felt the need for some wise words from my dear old Dad.

"Since when did 'life' become interchangeable with 'career'?" Dad griped. "It seems to me you've spent your whole life trying to fill a gap – to make your mark. The problem is you believe your purpose *is* your career."

He leaned forward, put his hand on my leg.

"Life's not a career, Kim," he said quietly. "A career is just a job. Life's more like your Tai Chi. It's perpetual motion – there are no gaps."

I thought about that for a bit, hiding my confusion in my beer.

"So what did you do next?" Dad prompted after a little while.

"What I always do when adversity strikes," I smiled at him. "I took a trip."

"India?" Dad looked at me wryly. "And now you're here."

"Well, I couldn't pass up the opportunity to make a difference, to find something meaningful to do with my life," I explained. "I needed to dust off my corporate scars and, besides, all my writing seemed to lead me to India."

"And then it seemed important to see you," I added.

"And? Did you find what you were looking for?" He asked.

"Nope!" I replied. As the enormity of that statement dawned on me, my eyes began to swell.

"Hey, what's wrong?" he said.

"I don't know Dad," I exhaled. "Sometimes I feel as if my life's not my own."

"What do you mean?" he asked with a soft compassion.

"I've lived and loved but nothing seems to stick," I said sniffling. "Each direction I go in I'm scuppered through no fault of my own. I just don't know what to do. I'm tired of trying and tired of being strong. With all the moves I've had it's as if I were possessed, driven towards god knows what — and I'm fearful of what's in my future."

"And what is it that you really want, Kim?" he asked.

"I don't know!" I cried out in frustration, trying to explain it to him. "It's on the tip of my tongue but it always eludes me. Just when I think I'm getting close to something real, something

I want, it spirals away and I head off in another direction. Why Dad? Why can't I ever find it?"

I'd secretly hoped my dad would step up to the paternal plate. I'd always felt lucky to receive my grandparent's wisdom. Although I was never keen to listen to Mum's two cents, I felt I'd always missed out on good fatherly advice. Dad had been too young and too inexperienced to offer me anything when I was a teenager.

"You've always had an inquisitive mind. You were always searching for something," he said gently. "Did you ever stop to think that living like a whirling dervish doesn't work?"

"You say you want a home, somewhere to belong," he went on as I hung on each and every word. "But maybe the scene was set for you when you were a kid? You changed schools a hell of a lot as I recall – and each time you just went along, like a trooper. You knuckled down and fitted in as if nothing had happened. I assumed you were happy enough, but maybe I was wrong."

"It was never the same after we moved from St. Albans to the pub," I agreed tearfully. "I was really desperate not to leave but I had no say in the fact my life was being ripped apart. It was the same when you and Mum divorced. Thinking about it now, that same feeling of something important being whipped away has haunted me all my life."

I hadn't known it was true until I said it out loud. All those wonderful opportunities that had seemed like dreams come true had been ripped away from me at the last minute – a relationship with Dougal, a purpose in Venezuela and with UNESCO, a chance at building a home in New Zealand and Melbourne. Then to top it off it was too late to have my own family. And I realised I was deeply afraid to find out what I'd lose next.

"I'm so sorry, Kim. I had no idea," Dad said taking my hand. "Maybe that's why you keep moving now – so you never feel that way again. If you don't get too attached to anything then maybe you won't feel so desperate when you have to leave?"

I looked at him in wonder. "Do you really think it's that simple?" I asked.

"That simple and that complicated," he shrugged. "If there's one thing I've learned in my travels, it's that seekers seek. They don't know how to do anything else.

"So you think there's no hope? I'll never find my home?" I asked, a little annoyed. "I should get used to it, is that what you're saying?"

"No. I'm saying, know your needs," he replied softly, letting go of my hand. "Be a finder not a seeker. Stay focused on the present and stop chasing around the world – or you could be running forever."

"So you think the secret to life is plugging in and connecting to the now?" I asked.

"Yes," he replied. "Live life like your Tai Chi – in perpetual motion but slow and precise, with conscious intent?"

A wave of peace flew over me. The clouds parted and I smiled.

"Wow, Dad – where were you all those missing years? I could have done with your wisdom a long time ago," I laughed.

"We all have our lessons to learn Kim," he replied, looking me in the eyes. "Some of us are just slower learners than others."

"Cheers to that," I said, raising my glass.

"To living life as a finder," he replied, raising his own beer. We sat in silence for a while, each with our own thoughts. Dad finally harrumphed.

"On a positive note," he said. "It seems to me you've done well." At my questioning glance and wry smirk, he continued, tapping his finger on the bar top.

"You've seen much of what the world has to offer – and you've done it in style. You've experienced a multitude of cultures and countries. And you've managed to maintain an alternative lifestyle," he surmised. "Isn't that exactly what you set out to achieve?"

I laughed raucously. "Yes. I suppose you're right. It's not what I'd expected though."

"But …" he added. 'There's always a but', I thought. "There's definitely something missing in your life. It seems to me you've always sacrificed love for home and purpose. And if there's anything I've learned it's life's not worth much without love."

"You know," he sighed. "It wasn't until I found love again that my purpose *found me*."

"And what is it, Dad?" I asked, curious.

"Ah! That would be telling," he replied. "I'd rather you discover it for yourself first. But what I will say is this – as far as I'm aware, none of the great books talk of a purpose, or having a job to do."

"Thanks," I replied sarcastically, adding, 'for nothing' in my head.

"If you haven't already, read Kipling's' *If*. It might help," he said, cryptically.

I signalled to the barman again.

"It's great listening to you two," he said as he poured us another round. "We never believe half his stories, but now we know they're probably true." I laughed. Dad winked and turned to the room with his lopsided grin. With a start I realised he probably knew everyone in this bar better than he knew me.

"What happened to that Scotsman? I forget his name now," Dad said suddenly.

"You mean Dougal?" I asked, surprised. I'd completely forgotten Dad had briefly met Dougal when we'd crossed paths with him at a pub in my old hometown. In fact, that was the last time we'd shared a beer.

"You seemed so happy together – a perfect fit!" He

remembered. "I saw how he looked at you, and how you followed his every move. The two of you were truly connected."

In that very moment, I knew – the world couldn't be my playground forever. I had to settle down somewhere. Find love and you'll find purpose – Dad's words echoed through my brain. And suddenly I understood exactly what to do.

"Glasgow," I said, smiling from ear to ear. "After Christmas I'll go home to my beloved Glasgow." Perhaps I'd look up Dougal while I was there.

"And that's our cue. I'm afraid if you want to make your boat it's time for us to leave…" He said looking as if he wished it weren't so.

I glanced down at my watch. Late for pick-ups, in the nick of time for drop-offs – that's how my family works. Just enough time for one last beer?

Comfortably perched on bar stools, I hung on to the moment, not wanting it to end. As my Dad's eyes left me, flicking to the clock above the door, it dawned on me that I finally understood what I'd been searching for! And Glasgow wasn't going anywhere anytime soon.

"Want another one?" I asked.

"You'll miss your boat," Dad replied.

I turned to the barman without further thought:

"Two beers. Please."

"A chip off the old block, eh!" The barman said, shaking his head as cheers erupted from the bar.

And neither Dad nor I could wipe the silly grins off our faces.

===><===

12

THE HIGHLANDS

Christmas Eve. I'd only been at my sister's less than twenty-four hours when a LinkedIn message arrived from Dougal.

"Can't believe I came across your details," it read.

"Have you got friends in immigration?" I replied. "I just arrived at Heathrow. I'll be in Glasgow next week. Want to meet?"

I'd ended up staying a week with Dad to catch up. We laughed and talked and it was with a heavy heart (and the promise of a return visit) that I'd left for the UK.

When I touched down on New Years Eve, the Scottish sky was clear and blue, the light bright and it was bitterly cold — but I didn't care. I was brimming with excitement to be in my dearly beloved Glasgow and meet up with Dougal again.

I booked myself into an old favourite hotel – the Grosvenor in the West End. It was Hogmanay — NYE, Scot-style. It was the biggest day in the Scottish festive calendar, probably because Christmas Day had been effectively banned for four hundred years during the Protestant Reformation (in fact, it only became a public holiday in 1958, while Boxing Day had to wait until 1974). It is also a long celebration — it starts on New

Year's Eve and continues to January 2. Many Scots still observe the Hogmanay traditions, including cleaning the house, singing Auld Lang Syne as the bells chime on the strike of midnight and — the most popular — First-Footing, where the first person to enter the house after midnight (ideally a tall, dark man because once a blond stranger arriving on your doorstep meant a Viking raid) brings gifts of salt, coal and a dram (whisky) to bring good fortune to the household throughout the ensuing year.

Feeling energised, I had to get out and explore my beloved city. I was curious to know if anything had changed. I wandered the deserted, frosty streets. I reminisced over the old days, rediscovering my old haunts. I dropped into a café I once frequented and was chuffed when the waiter remembered my order – chicken liver pate with homemade oatcakes – after so many years. I washed down my meal with a cool crisp glass of Pouilly-Fumé, remembering the first bottle I'd shared with Dougal. It was great to be home.

The mini bar options weren't to my liking, so I called room service for a bottle of bubbles thinking I'd toast the new year and send well wishes to Dougal as I had done every year since we met. A gentle rat-a-tat-tat came on the hotel room door.

It was the man himself, my own dark stranger to darken my doorstep on the first of a new year – in his hand not salt, coal and a dram but my favourite shortbread, a bottle of bubbles and a single yellow rose.

=><=

Entangled we woke to a cold, cold New Years Day.

'Am I really home?' I muttered, to myself. The night before was a whirlwind of emotion. We couldn't get enough of each other – the little grips and gentle tugs suggesting 'you're mine – I'm so happy to have you'. Cheeky winks and affirmative nods, we caught each other's sideways glances, we finished each other's sentences.

"How could it be true?" I murmured. Our enthusiasm for each other hadn't wavered – even after seventeen years. I looked over at the older man lying next to me, still recognisably the young man I fell for in the shadow of Uluru.

=><=

We spent three superb days catching up on the years — deaths, births, marriages and divorce, studies, careers, jobs, friends, family, and travels — a tsunami had been under the bridge. We laughed and commiserated, told each other of trials and tribulations. We mused over how our lives had turned out — and how our paths had now crossed. We joked at the 'what ifs', 'whys' and 'wherefores'. Who needed an excuse to stay huddled in the warmth of a long lost love?

"Hmmm," he wondered sleepily. "What year were we up to? 1995 – did you get your degree?"

"Yes. I did actually," I said, sarcastically. I figured little had changed; I knew the rejoinder.

"So, you finally finished something," he teased. "And did you get your dream job?"

"No. Unfortunately not," I explained. "Nothing much went to plan after that, really. I ended up back in finance for a while. Then, one day I'd had enough. I wanted a better life. So, I left for Australia."

"Really?" Dougal nudged me. "I'd heard it was South America."

"Well – you heard right. But that was later," I said. "Do you remember when we walked along the shores of Connemara?"

"How could I ever forget?" he laughed. "It was crazy – fighting that gale force wind in those stupid, bright green 'penis head' ponchos!"

"Well, it feels like I've been battling that wind ever since," I explained. "Each time it got too stormy, I felt I had to move somewhere new." Like Madam Chocolate I'd get a feeling. Then the wind would blow and before I knew it I was packing my bags and making tracks. It's like my strings were pulled and I had no choice but to go.

"It sounds very unsettling," he said.

"Yes, at first it is, but then it was exciting never knowing what life would have in store," I shrugged. "And now I'm beat. I've had enough of being on the move and I'm done with packing my bags."

"What if I pack your bags? Will you come away with me?" he asked, immediately clarifying, "Actually, what I mean is – would you like to go away for a few days to get to know each other, again? To re-connect properly?"

'He's still a dream', I thought. 'Quite the opposite of Charles.'

"Ever thoughtful," I said. "I'd love to. Where shall we go?" Stepping in for a bear hug, I whispered, "Not camping?"

"If you don't mind, I'd like to make the arrangements a surprise," he tried to say, before I planted my lips on his.

=><=

"Ah! You're a star," I called, in delight, "The Tormaukin Hotel." One of our old regulars – an 18th Century Drover's Inn filled with rustic charm in the foot of Perthshire's Ochil Hills, the heartland of Scotland. Our cute and romantic room had retained some of the original features of a countryside hotel. Perfect. Checked-in, settled-in, we took to the bar.

Slouched in the high backed, leather armchairs, set beside the roaring log fire we sampled the local craft beer, as we exchanged stories about our South American travels, waiting for our table.

"Your table's ready. If you'd like to make your way to the conservatory," said the Maître D', with a friendly smile.

"After you," Dougal said, with a beautiful smile, taking my waist, he indicated for me to lead the way. A true gent - nothing had changed. I followed the Maître D' to the perfectly positioned table, front row in the conservatory bay, overlooking the Glendevon Valley.

"Is this suitable for you, Madam?" asked the Maître D', flapping the white linen napkin, for my lap. "I believe you've ordered a Sancerre, Sir?" he said, seeking confirmation. "I'll bring it right away."

It took us a while to decide what to eat – too many delectable dishes, and too much conversation.

"Are you ready to order?" asked the waitress.

"Entrée. I'll have the Scottish black pudding, with scallops and mousse," please.

"And for you, Sir," asked the young lady.

"The same for me, please," he said, with a glance to me. I knew what he was thinking. I was thinking it too.

"And for your main, Madam?"

"The crusted, rainbow trout, please," I said looking at Dougal, with a cheeky grin, as the waitress marked her pad.

"Sir?"

"Make that two, please. And we'll have sides of dauphinoise potatoes, and seasonal vegetables," he said, looking to me for approval. Which he knew he already had.

Adjacent, we sat at the small square table, hand in hand, deep in conversation. We laughed and teased, told tales and recalled old times, sparking each others' thoughts. Together we were just as we'd always been, an incorrigible pair of hedonists.

"So, tell me about Australia. Has it changed?" he said. I told him how I'd lost my job and despaired of ever finding my purpose.

"What did you do?"

"Come on!" I said, spurring him to think, " – you know!"

"You went travelling of course," he laughed, realising it was unlikely I'd have done much else. "India?"

"The Mighty Murray!" I shook my head, grinning at him.

"Our Murray?" he asked with a childlike surprise. "You went without me?"

"Indeed. I did. But let me tell you where else I went without you," I replied. "You'll be glad you weren't there."

"Where?" he asked dramatically.

"The Alice!" I cried.

My return to the Alice was not without reservation. The memories from my previous visit to the Rock some twenty-nine years before were so very precious to me. Was I prepared to risk them being replaced by something potentially quite ordinary? I'd heard stories of the Red Centre as a modern tourist destination, a far cry from the spiritual home of the indigenous Australians I'd experienced. I understood they'd sold out to the mighty dollar. My immediate reaction to the thought that I should visit sent shudders down my spine — it was inconceivable I would return. But I'll admit I was curious.

I'd headed straight to Uluru in a rented Nissan X-Trail, exploring as I progressed. My accommodation was near King's Canyon — a camel farm where I stayed one night under canvas.

"It wasn't quite the same as being with you on the Mighty Murray, under the expanse of clear sky hosting billions of little white specks," I said, sadly. "Do you remember how we mimicked cockatoos and kookaburras at dawn and dusk?"

"Go on" he said with a wink. "I know it's hard for you to resist. Give me a 'Kookaburra sits in the old gum tree' for old times sake."

At that moment, the waiter came to escort us over to the fireside for digestives. We sunk into the big old comfortable chairs, each watching the flames reduce to a sensual flicker as the evening wore on. Dougal ordered a dram – single malt for himself and Armagnac for me.

"Tell me more about your red road trip," Dougal said, taking great interest.

The next morning I was riding off into the outback high on the back of a stinky single-humped friend. The air was still cool, the trail dusty and the scrub yet to show signs of life. Swaying from one side to the other, the camel waddled half asleep with its beautiful long eyelashes until the wildflowers appeared. Stopping without command, my trusted friend rocked – forward, backward, forward again – until he settled on the ground for me to alight. As breakfast was laid, I listened intently to our guide talk about the desert, its ecosystems and how it was settled. He answered questions about the camels and their drivers, and spoke of the role they played in the early pioneering days.

"Did you know that Australia has cameleers?" I asked Dougal, my eyes bright. I relayed how we'd been told about Abdul Wade, who'd arrived Australia in 1879, initially working for two Afghan brothers before importing his own camels and recruiting Afghan cameleers for the recently formed Bourke Camel Carrying Co. In 1903, Wade purchased the Wangamanna station in New South Wales, living there with his wife and seven children. At the height of his success, Wade had four hundred camels and sixty men working for him. Respected by his employees and nicknamed the 'Afghan prince', he worked hard at being seen as an equal by his Australian peers. He dressed as a European, educated his children at top private schools and even became a naturalised citizen. But success in Australian society eluded him and his attempts to fit in were ridiculed. At the end of the camel era, Wade sold his station and returned to Afghanistan, surrendering his Australian passport.

"I can't help but see myself as one of Wade's camels," I mused to Dougal, who laughed uproariously. "No. Wait! Hear me out!" I started counting out the reasons on my fingers.

"My expeditions often end in disaster. I often feel drawn to, but ultimately lost in, foreign lands. Okay, I'm not a cheap beast of burden but I have been called upon to avert corporate disaster as a consequence of my reliability, resilience and ability to survive in the face of adversity," I said.

"Don't forget you look remarkably like a camel, too," he joked. I made a face.

"I haven't finished," I kept on. "Four, I'm constantly driven by other people's needs rather than my own – and five – no one seems to know how to handle me."

"Until now," Dougal interjected. Smiling softly at him, I paused to savour the moment.

"I'd always thought I fit in everywhere, but belonged nowhere," I mused. "Ultimately, though my return to the Alice showed me I actually fit nowhere but belong everywhere."

"So you carry your culture with you?" he asked, getting it.

"Exactly!" I dearly loved this man.

"One for the road?" Dougal asked, raising his glass to the barman to indicate another round then rising to stand. "Let's take them upstairs."

$$= > < =$$

We snuggled in under the soft, cotton sheets, warm and cosy on the wild, windy Scottish winter night.

"Any new scars?" I asked Dougal in a soft, tired voice.

"Plenty," he grimaced. Taking my finger, he raised it to his face. We laughed thinking about the first time we'd met on the other side of the world, under the stars.

"What next? Where do we go from here?" Dougal took the first step. And I felt I owed it to tell him the whole truth about me.

"Remember that night we went for pizza? When you'd thought I had a stroke?" I asked. He looked confused, nodded.

"Well, you were right – sort of," I continued. "Dougal, I have MS."

We both fell silent. I could tell I'd stopped him in his tracks.

"When were you diagnosed?" He asked, breaking our comfortable silence.

"After Holland. Before Canada," I replied.

"Why on earth didn't you tell me?" he asked.

"I wanted to – but it didn't seem appropriate. I didn't want to spoil our short time together," I explained.

"Oh Kim! I'm so sorry. How devastating for you," he said, with a saddened face. "But you look a million dollars! I can't quite believe it."

"No worries. It's not really something I think about too often," I explained. "I've been so lucky really." I told him how I'd decided not to let MS rule my life. I wasn't going to sit around and wait for it to collect – I had dreams. Never in denial, despite what others said, I acknowledged the condition and managed it my way and without relying on drugs. I had wings on my feet and they needed to fly.

We were silent again for a few moments.

"I'm so proud of you," he said, pulling me closer and holding me tight. "You've done well."

"Do I still have the last quarter inch at the bottom of your heart?" I whispered.

With an endearing smile he nodded, "Yes."

===><===

EPILOGUE
THE LAST STAND

My legs weren't responding quite as they should – my reaction times were a little slower and they seemed to catch underfoot when I lifted them. It might have been my imagination but it was as if the sensations in my legs were a bit more muted. It had been eleven years since I'd had a major attack – a minor miracle, I thought. Still, after talking over it with Dougal, I decided to get Dr Harriette to do spine and brain scans. With my new life in Glasgow about to begin I wanted to make sure everything was going well. I wasn't too concerned.

So it was a bit of a shock to get a message to call Dr Harriette.

Dr Harriette welcomed me as though I were the only thing in the world that mattered; she hadn't changed a bit.

"I was just reading your file. I can't believe how long it's been," she said, as I entered the room, "You look amazing." She focused intently on me, looking for any tell tale signs of facial weakness.

Brief niceties followed. Working? Not at the moment. Settled? Not at the moment. And, how have you been?

"Fantastic," I replied. "Just wanted to check in – find out where the disease is at, you know."

"Indeed. Well, I've had a good look at your suite of scans and I think there's a few things you should see," she said, turning her monitor in my direction.

My heart dropped. Those words were too familiar. I tried to follow Dr Harriette's voice as she methodically scrolled through a series of images, pointing to areas of interest.

"Surely I'm in remission?" I interrupted. "I mean, I feel great – how can anything be wrong?"

"Kim, I think it's time we talked," she said. "There's no such thing as remission for MS – it will stay active all your life and can get worse at any time."

"You're clearly one of the lucky ones – around a third of those with MS go through life without any persistent disability, and suffer only intermittent, transient episodes," she went on to explain. I'd heard it before, all those years ago, but I'd long since forgotten.

"Regardless, eighty-five per cent end up with secondary progressive MS – where you'll have more chronic attacks and you'll bounce back much less completely so that we see a pattern of steady deterioration rather than episodic flares," Dr Harriette told me. "We need to prepare for that eventuality."

"It's time to talk about taking drugs," she said, putting her hand up to still what she could see was a protest from me. "I know you're not a fan, but you really need to consider them."

I questioned her intently as she drew diagrams, gave recommendations for reading and discussed what drugs she wanted me to take and their possible side effects. Then she passed me a website address and a password.

"Go do your research, come back to me with your preferred drug option and we'll get you started," she said with a note of finality.

Numbed by her words, I gathered together my pieces of paper and reached for the door.

"I just can't believe it – look at you!" Dr Harriette said as I opened it. "Imagine if you'd taken the drugs eleven years ago! The pharmaceutical companies would proclaim you a complete success."

=><=

All afternoon I lay on my hotel bed, gutted and unable to move – except to blow my nose. I bawled. I bargained. I was distraught. Of course, I'd known about this possibility for nigh on thirty years but I'd always been sure I'd beat it. I'd got on with my life, determined to grab every possible opportunity, sensation and experience the world had to offer, without a puff for my MS, except when it threatened to collect. I'd travelled full circle around the world and here I was again, right back where I started.

And where had that long road taken me? I still had no home. No purpose. I'd found love again, but if I lost the use of my legs, would I keep it? How long did I have till my luck ran out?

By morning I was defiant. I showered, packed a backpack and got in my hire car. I turned off my phone and just drove. I went west on the A82, heading towards Fort William. In a few hours I could be at the foot of Ben Nevis, Scotland's tallest mountain. I'd planned to climb the Ben years ago but never quite got around to it. Now it seemed the only thing that mattered to me – as if I was determined to prove to the world that my legs were still good to go. There was also a whiff of bolshiness – master the most difficult challenges straight away, I thought to myself. The smaller ones can wait. Ultimately, it was just another way to distract myself from the anguish I felt: I needed to do something – anything – but sit in my room and cry.

It wasn't until I was hugging the banks of Loch Lomond, my arm out the window capturing the cool breeze, that I began to relax a little. I surprised myself by frivolously humming, "By yon bonnie banks and by yon bonnie braes…" remembering that my own true love and I had once stopped at the tranquil water's edge, mesmerised by the reflections of Ben Lomond's dramatic summit. If Dougal were here, I mused, we'd probably take a wee dram at The Drovers Inn at the head of the loch.

"O ye'll tak' the high road, and I'll tak' the low road," I sang on, thinking about the journey I'd taken and the one that was ahead. I'd definitely taken the long road – and it had taught me much. But I was coming to its end now and I wondered – was it time to take the high road?

As I continued around the head of the Gareloch towards Glen Coe, the landscape began to change. I crossed the Rest And Be Thankful, named because the original road out of Glen Coe was so long and steep that it was tradition for travellers to rest at the top and be thankful for having reached the highest point. For once I couldn't think of anything I was thankful for – paradoxically at this high point in the road I was at my lowest ebb.

Suddenly, the road dropped away to reveal the most magnificent Glen – and it was like I'd come home at last. The scene before me was that familiar I could have wept. And in that moment I knew why I was driving. I was revisiting happier times, wanting to recapture something of what I had once shared with Dougal all those years ago. I was tempted to stop a dozen times – to revisit our old haunts – but still I let the road carry me higher and higher toward the heavens.

And as I climbed so did my spirit.

I reached the base of the Ben around lunchtime. Making my way through the low-lying thicket to the start of the rocky trail, I doggedly began on my way, feeling quite jolly despite the mist. I shimmied across a bridge more like a fallen telegraph pole to the slippery bank on the other side. With limited space to manoeuvre, I grabbed some protruding roots — one large heave had me positioned, foot steadied and on hard ground. Then my ascent began in earnest, through narrow, awkward gully stairways cut between embankments lined with sharp jutting pale grey rocks and streams and gently flowing brooks, where small ferns and heathers rooted amongst the crevices.

Soon the stream had become a torrent of ice-cold water that coursed its way from the summit. It took more effort to climb – the trail was steeper and rockier underfoot. I huffed and panted, single-mindedly pushing myself forward, unwavering in my resolve to reach the top.

And then I was there. Across a huge stony plateau I made my way to the cairn that marks Ben Nevis' highest point. Breathing raggedly, I looked back along the road I'd come, stretching all the way down to Ben Lomond. Remarkably, there was no one in sight, no tourist to share my victory.

It was then that I heard it. A lone piper's call. He stood below me, still one thousand feet above the great wilderness of Rannoch – The Flower of Scotland. It was probably the exhaustion talking but the sound ignited something raw inside. And in that moment, I felt at one, as though I didn't really exist — it was breathtaking. Eyes wet with an indescribable joy, I burst into song, accompanying the bagpipes at the top of my voice: When will we see/ Your like again/ That fought and died for/ Your wee bit o' Hill and Glen.

As the sound died away, I felt completely and utterly one with the dark, majestic mountain, transported out of my body into the universe, where time and space stood still. Mesmerised by the power and purity, with an uplifting sense that nature knows best, I felt cocooned, bathed in an immensely delightful satisfaction. Just as quickly, everything seemed perfectly clear. I could see every step of the road I'd taken – and at last I was grateful. I knew, without a doubt, that though I'd never felt a sense of place, I was my own home. I'd felt my way around the world, gathering experiences and trusting my instincts. I'd been alone but rarely lonely. I'd seen amazing, unbelievable things and spoken to incredible people from all walks of life. I'd gazed in disbelief at some of the most sensational, architectural marvels in places you'd think impossible to reach – let alone build. I'd stood in awe of the tens of thousands of labourers and master tradesmen (willing or otherwise), working for decades on monuments, palaces, kingdoms, towns, and grand cities.

However, nomads like me have no time for mastery – we're driven by the wind and we're always on the move. And that was okay, the Ben seemed to tell me. The earth is a giant playground full of wonders and thrills and we each have our ways of getting to our journey's end. Life's road is long. But it's no smooth, fast track superhighway. Rather, it's an endless stretch of cobbled streets that leave you teetering all the way. Plus, there's no definitive map. One minute you feel safe and secure. You pick up speed. And then the unexpected… jerks you back to reality. You stumble, pick yourself up, refocus, and move hesitantly forward again, watching where you put your feet. And before you know, you're hurtling again, but this time with a different perspective.

I'd thought such disruptions only a nuisance. They'd seemed to come at the most inopportune moments. I wanted to bridge them, ford them, fill them in with the white noise of striving towards a goal that always seemed just out of reach. But there, with that craggy old mountain as my witness, I finally made my peace with them. Because I knew, abruptly, that real life happened in those re-directs. They weren't trials, but something to be treasured. They'd given me a chance to experience the remarkable things this world had to offer – whether it was five-star hotels or mice-ridden backpacker hostels, Michelin star restaurants or coypu cafés, natural wonders like Uluru or the exquisitely man-made Taj Mahal. Without them I'd never have taken up the opportunity to do whatever took my fancy – explore, experiment, and evolve.

Looking back in that second at my life's story, I saw it was only during my travels that I was ever truly 'me'; my high energy and devil demon in perfect harmony. Don't get me wrong; it wasn't all a bed of roses. The road challenged me in more ways than I could have ever have imagined and I learned more than any classroom could have ever taught. What's more, I survived. Like a Balinese temple moulded by the battering sea, it was the challenges that shaped me – they made me more confident, resilient, and resourceful, taught me how to trust my gut and feel my way through life's ups and downs.

It's said that memories are better than dreams – dreams can be broken but memories are forever. Negotiating life's gaps had given me so many wonderful memories. Travel had opened my mind, in turn teaching me how to open my heart to friends and family. I'd set off in search of 'my culture', and ended up looking for 'a place to belong'. I'd believed finding a place to call 'home' would mean I'd no longer need to search. I could rest and just 'be'. But, as my Dad had taught me, a seeker's job was simply that – to seek. By definition, we never stay still and we never find what we're looking for – it's just not in our job description.

All this took just seconds to see – like it had been spontaneously downloaded into my brain. I smiled to see that my seeking had offered me ample time to trace the patterns of my life, to understand how often history repeats until I caught a glimpse of what I was really travelling towards. I'd thought I'd been searching for a place to belong; in fact, it was the seven-year-old me who had been searching everywhere for love so she could know her true purpose in life – to be resolutely herself.

And there I stood, at the top of the world, in sublime stillness yet electrified by the formidable power of the colossal, distant, snow-covered mountains, knowing — indisputably –

    — the world was still all mine for the taking*!*

        ===><===

"He who travels much learns more
than he who lives long."

Old Arab proverb

***If** you can keep your head when all about you*
Are losing theirs and blaming it on you;
If you can trust yourself when all men doubt you,
But make allowances for their doubting too;
If you can wait and not be tired by waiting,
Or, being lied about, don't deal in lies,
Or, being hated, don't give way to hating,
And yet don't look too good, nor talk too wise;
If you can dream - and not make dream your master;
If you can think - and not make thoughts your aim;
If you can meet with triumph and disaster
And treat those two imposters the same;
If you can bear to hear the truth you've spoken
Twisted by knaves to make a trap for fools,
Or watch the things you gave your life to broken,
And stoop and build 'em up with worn out tools;
If you can make one heap of all your winnings
And risk it on one turn of pitch-and-toss,
And lose, and start again at your beginnings
And never breathe a word about your loss;
If you can force your heart and nerve and sinew
To serve your turn long after they are gone,
And so hold on when there is nothing in you
Except the Will which says to them; "Hold on";
If you can talk with crowds and keep your virtue,
Or walk with kings - nor lose the common touch;
If neither foes nor loving friends can hurt you;
If all men count with you, but none too much;
If you can fill the unforgiving minute
With sixty seconds' worth of distance run -
Yours is the Earth and everything that's in it,
And - which is more - you'll be a Man, my son!
Rudyard Kipling

A Note from the Author

Despite being successful in my 'career', friends and colleagues have occasionally offered unsolicited suggestions as to what I should do. I've rebuked none of these suggestions – in fact, I'd go so far to say they often resonated with me. I had no idea why more to the point, what or whom I'd mentor/write about/give guidance on/design. But I did know I had far more to offer than my so-called professional skills.

And therein lies the creation of my cheeky chimp friend, Scratch. He began life as a columnist in Australia. He positively delights in offering an alternative perspective on his readers' dilemmas, and he's often likened to Dorothy Dicks; he's what the Brits would call an 'agony aunt'. Scratch is a curious, inquisitive fellow with a rebellious streak. He likes to solve complex problems and disrupt things for the greater good.

If you'd like to know more about Scratch, pay me a visit on social media or somewhere on the cobblestones at, https://KimVenskunas.com while you wait for our next publication.

— Kim Venskunas, September 2018

"BON VOYAGE, MY FRIEND."

Don't forget the postcards!
We'd love to hear from you.

Kim & Scratch

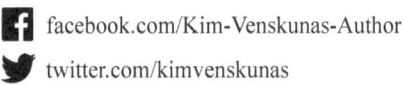

facebook.com/Kim-Venskunas-Author
twitter.com/kimvenskunas

Acknowledgments

Last, but not least – time to say a huge THANK YOU to those who helped me deliver *The Gap* as an independent author and publisher.

Not only has travelling life's cobblestones been fraught with discovery, roadblocks, excitement and disappointments, so has the process of producing my very personal story, for publication. I've been on a pretty steep learning curve, facilitated by many employees of company's, to which I gave no business.

For that, I acknowledge those below who have to varying degrees encouraged, supported or simply helped increase my knowledge, defiance or determination to do things my way.

Thank You, to The Society of Authors; ALLi - Alliance of Independent Authors; my editor and confident, Felicity Van Rysbergen of Well Versed Copywriting; the cover designer, Henry Hyde; Ben's team at Cameron Publicity & Marketing; Matador Publishing; Mirador Publishing; SilverWood Books and IngramSpark.

And, of course it goes without saying a special thank you to my friends and family, who have also been on much of this journey, with me – perhaps too much, at times? Sorry.

Yours Truly,
Kim Venskunas

www.ingramcontent.com/pod-product-compliance
Lightning Source LLC
Chambersburg PA
CBHW020647300426
44112CB00007B/273